THE
WRITER
IN THE
SOUTH

THE
WRITER
IN THE
SOUTH

Studies in a Literary Community

LOUIS D. RUBIN, JR.

*MERCER UNIVERSITY LAMAR
MEMORIAL LECTURES, NO. 15*

UNIVERSITY OF GEORGIA PRESS

ATHENS

To Julia Randall

"Thou art not of the fashion of these times,
Where none will sweat but for promotion ..."

©

1972

UNIVERSITY OF GEORGIA PRESS

LC 72–78045

ISBN 0–8203–0289–9

Printed in the United States of America

Contents

Foreword

"LET THE LAMP AFFIX ITS BEAM," WALLACE STEVENS'S AD-
juration in his famous poem, "The Emperor of Ice Cream,"
might well be used to describe the three areas Louis D.
Rubin, Jr., discussed in his series of lectures on *The Writer
in the South.* Into realms of southern literature that had
been heretofore poorly illuminated, or that were often
even dark, he focused the lamp of his scholarship and
showed why much early southern writing was necessarily
polemical, why a person would have to be born there fully
to understand the South, and why and how the southern
renascence in literature occurred. To a long list of distinguished predecessors—fourteen to be exact—who have par-
ticipated in the Eugenia Dorothy Blount Lamar lecture
series at Mercer University, Professor Rubin brought
added luster. As a native southerner, born in Charleston,
South Carolina, and educated in the South, he knew well
into what corners he should shine his light.

Southern writing has been too little known by the great
body of American readers, even by southern readers. But
the history of American literature in the last fifty years has
in very large measure been the history of southern literature. Until recently, however, southern writing has not received the attention, understanding, or appreciation it so
richly deserves. That such belated recognition has come at
all is due not only to the excellence of such southern writers as Ellen Glasgow, Thomas Wolfe, William Faulkner,

Flannery O'Connor, and a host of others, but also to the scholarly research and criticism done by sound and solid students of southern literature—notably men like Professor Rubin.

Dr. Rubin attended the College of Charleston, the University of Richmond, where he received his A.B., and Johns Hopkins University, where he earned his M.A. and Ph.D. degrees. Now professor of English at the University of North Carolina, he has published numerous books, written a novel, been editor or coeditor of several literary journals. He is also the editor of the prestigious volume *A Bibliographical Guide to the Study of Southern Literature*—a comprehensive and extremely valuable work.

The Lamar Lectures Committee, the Mercer community, and those in the entire contiguous area are deeply grateful to Eugenia Dorothy Blount Lamar, whose magnanimity made the lectures possible in perpetuity. The committee also thinks that Professor Rubin's lectures eminently satisfied the stipulation in Mrs. Lamar's bequest: "to provide lectures of the very highest type of scholarship which will aid in the permanent preservation of the values of southern culture, history, and literature." With the glow of native understanding and the brilliant candlepower of literary discernment, Professor Rubin did indeed "let the lamp affix its beam."

> John E. Byron
> For the Lamar Lectures Committee

Mercer University
Macon, Georgia

Preface

SOME TWENTY YEARS BEFORE THESE LECTURES ON THE
Writer in the South were prepared for delivery at Mercer
University, there was announced in the *Hopkins Review,*
a journal of which I was coeditor, the forthcoming publication of a symposium of modern southern literature, in
which "an attempt will be made to evaluate southern writing since the first world war, including its major participants, its background, and its relationship to other writing
of the same period." The result of that enterprise was a
book, entitled *Southern Renascence,* which is still in print,
and also the demise of the *Hopkins Review,* which foun-
dered under the weight of what quickly proved to be an
overabundance of publishable material. In the two decades
that have since ensued, however, I have continued to think
about and write about the South and its writers, both the
moderns and their forebears, and so when the invitation
came to deliver the Lamar Lectures for 1971, I saw the
occasion as an opportunity to try to sort out for myself some
first principles. I had spent a good deal of time, and used
up a goodly amount of printer's ink, discoursing on the relationship of various southern writers to the South. Well,
what was that relationship? What had been, and what now
was, the place of the writer in the South? What had the fact
of his residence in the southern states to do with the way
that he wrote? If the South had changed, how had the
change affected the southern writer? What were some of

the differences in the ways that being a southerner affected the work of, say, William Gilmore Simms, and the ways in which it affected that of William Faulkner? And if, as I had always felt, the southern origins of Mark Twain had so much to do with the forms that his imagination took, then what was the relationship between the South and the work of Mark Twain? Not that I could hope to settle such questions, for in addition to my own intellectual limitations there was the obvious fact that these would be lectures, with the brevity and imprecision inherent in that form of discourse. Yet the very informality and tentativeness of the lecture format was appealing, as offering the chance to speculate, hypothesize, to move here and there, around and within the subject as one chose, without the necessity that more formal and extended inquiry might force upon me to document and establish everything I said and to cover all aspects of the subject. Informality, after all, has its advantages. I once wrote an essay on *The Turn of the Screw,* and I sent an offprint of it to a noted biographer of Henry James, who promptly responded by censuring the temerity of what he delicately termed "you hit-and-run guys" to write about one work by Henry James without taking into consideration all the other works. Presumably I too should have been writing a five-volume biography before daring to express myself in print on the matter. Well, a lecture is by its very nature a hit-and-run affair; and that, after twenty years of detailed involvement with the literature of the South, is what I wanted now to do: to touch upon a few of the problems involved in the relationship of the southern writer to the South, and to suggest a few hypotheses.

The three lectures which follow are roughly chronological in their sequence. The first has to do with the writer in the Old South, the second with the post–Civil War South and Mark Twain, the third with the southern literary renascence that flowered beginning in the 1920s. But though they were written in that order, in inception they did not come about that way. They began with the incident related at the start of the third lecture, or more properly, with some speculations on what it meant. The incident happened more than fifteen years ago, appropriately enough as the culmination of a weekend spent in Macon, Georgia, at the first spring meeting of the Southeastern American Studies Association. I had thought about it from time to time in subsequent years, and the more I did so, the more it seemed to me to point to an important relationship of the southern writer to the South. For it involved a conception of community, and an attitude toward the availability of such a community, that I think lies at the heart of so much southern experience.

It was with this notion of a southern community in mind that I examine the relationship of the antebellum southern writer to the South. Here I have found it expedient to embark upon a lengthy digression from the concerns of literature proper. For if it was in the decades between 1820 and 1860 that the various southern states became the South, then it was in those years that the community identity must first have revealed itself. It seemed necessary, therefore, to attempt to take a look at what this community was, in order to understand the hold it exerted upon the writers, so that afterward I could trace the changes that the late nineteenth century and the twentieth century brought in the relationship of the southern writer to the southern community.

The second lecture, dealing with the local color period of the 1870s, 1880s, and 1890s, might appropriately have involved a study of just how the results of the Civil War and the Reconstruction affected the southern writer's attitude to his community. But I was confronted with something of a paradox, in that the only really major author of the late nineteenth-century South, Mark Twain, was not resident in the region after the war ended and his ties were

to the Old South rather than to the post-Appomattox region. The more I thought about it, however, the more I
became convinced that it was precisely because of this "paradox" that Mark Twain had been able to do what none of
the others ever really succeeded in doing: distance himself
from the allegiances of the southern community to the extent that he could look beneath the surface at the underlying values and attitudes of the society. And since a similar
capacity for perspective was what seemed to distinguish the
writers of the twentieth-century southern renascence from
the greater part of their predecessors, I have discussed
Mark Twain as, in effect, the first "modern" southern author.

The final lecture, naturally enough, focuses upon the
southern author of the post–World War I period, that of
the renascence, in which for the first time in the 150-year-
old history of the region so many of its authors achieved
a worldwide audience, for their stories and poems. Here I
faced a personal difficulty. For though logically I might be
expected to proceed to examine Faulkner, Wolfe, Warren,
Ransom, Tate, and their contemporaries in terms of the
community relationship I had been sketching for the nineteenth-century authors, the fact was that I had previously
gone after that topic on numerous occasions, and had even
written a full-length book, *The Faraway Country: Writers
of the Modern South,* about it. Other than a few new points
of emphasis, there was little that I might now hope to add
to what I had already had to say about Faulkner and the
others. Rather than attempt merely to recapitulate, therefore, I have centered my inquiry upon the specific topic of
the theoretical formulation of that community relationship, through the incident involving John Donald Wade
that had been my point of departure for the lectures, and
thus concentrate on the Agrarian symposium to which he
had been a contributor, *I'll Take My Stand.* That volume,

I felt, has ever since its publication in 1930 represented a kind of programmatic statement of the southern writer's involvement with his society, since though such authors as Faulkner, Thomas Wolfe, Eudora Welty, and others did not take part in it and were as often as not less than sympathetic to its specific counsels, much of what they had as writers to say about the South was implicit in its premises.

Such, in any event, is what I have sought to do in these lectures. I am all too aware of the inadequacy of the portrait here sketched. In dealing with the antebellum authors I have had very little to say about their writings, for I found it necessary to spend so much time sketching the society that I could not undertake any reasonable scrutiny of what they wrote about it. In the case of the postbellum writers, I have had to concentrate on Mark Twain to the exclusion of almost everyone else. It is with the twentieth-century writers, however, that I feel the largest burden of embarrassment. To begin with, I have completely ignored the instances of James Branch Cabell and Ellen Glasgow in Richmond. I have no excuse for this, except that what I might have said about their circumstance on this occasion (I have touched on the matter in a previous book) would have been essentially preliminary and introductory to the period of the post–World War I literary flowering, and it seemed the better use of time to focus upon the full spectacle itself. In concentrating on the Agrarians and on Faulkner, I have had to neglect, usually to the point of complete noninclusion, other important and good authors who might have been almost as appropriately discussed, and made equally as useful, I should say, to my thesis. And of course, in ending my explorations with the writers of the period between the wars, I have had nothing whatever to say about such post–World War II writers as Flannery O'Connor, William Styron, Carson McCullers, Walker Percy, and James Agee, to name five from among at least a dozen I should have liked to discuss. If my thesis has any validity—if what we have in the twentieth century has been a momentous distancing that afforded a perspective coming out of the divided allegiance of separation and identity—then the corollary seems implicit that the next generation of southern authors would not only move even further away, but would lose some of the artistic benefits residing in that clash of opposite styles of life. So that to leave that generation uninvestigated in my thesis is to leave the thesis without its latest chapter. But it would have required at least another lecture by itself to begin to do justice to that, and this, plus the suspicion that those who study southern literature are getting tired of hearing my meditations on the subject of Styron and his contemporaries, scared me off from it. Finally I have said absolutely nothing about an increasingly important aspect of the southern literary scene, the black southern writer. Here I think my neglect is more justifiable. For the black southern writer, whether he be Charles Chesnutt or James Weldon Johnson or Jean Toomer or Richard Wright or Ralph Ellison, obviously has been involved in a relationship to southern society and southern attitudes that is very different from that of the white southern author, so that my generalizations and suppositions about the community relationship would require a whole new kind of approach and examination. I should like to do that some day, but to tackle it in passing, in the course of three lectures, was more than might be ventured even by one not noted for prudence in refraining from rushing in where the angels know better than to tread.

I should like to express my gratitude to the faculty of Mercer University and to the trustees of the Eugenia Dorothy Blount Lamar Memorial Lectures for inviting me to deliver these lectures and then affording me so much hospitality during my visit. In particular I am indebted to Mr. Spencer B. King, Jr., Mr. Michael Cass, Mr. John E. Byron, Dean Garland F. Taylor, Miss May F. McMillan, and Mrs. Margaret Englehart. Mr. George Core has, as editor of the University of Georgia Press, given the text the close reading that under other circumstances I should have exacted of him as a friend. (In deference to Mr. Core and to the house style of the University of Georgia Press I have even suppressed my sense of outraged grammatical and sectional dignity and spelled both southern and southerner with a small "s.") My colleagues Lewis Leary, C. Hugh Holman, Blyden Jackson, and Carroll Hollis were inflicted with the task of reading the manuscript draft of these lectures, and all labored nobly to reform my barbarisms. Miss Jeanne Nostrandt and Miss Rosanne Coggeshall deciphered, typed, and retyped the text. Successive waves of graduate and undergraduate students in my seminars and classes at the University of North Carolina at Chapel Hill and at Hollins College, Virginia, have helped me to arrive at whatever insight into the subject under discussion these lectures may display.

Louis D. Rubin, Jr.

Chapel Hill, North Carolina
December 1, 1971

The Literary Community in the Old South

AT THE BEGINNING OF THAT BEST OF ALL NOVELS ABOUT the South, William Faulkner's *Absalom, Absalom!*, young Quentin Compson sits in the parlor of Miss Rosa Cold-field's house listening to an old woman telling a story. He is soon to leave Mississippi for his freshman year of college in the North, and is not sure why it is that Miss Rosa has asked him to come there that day. Miss Rosa herself feels it necessary to offer an excuse. "Because you are going away to attend the college at Harvard they tell me," she says. "So I dont imagine you will ever come back here and settle down as a country lawyer in a little town like Jefferson, since Northern people have already seen to it that there is little left in the South for a young man. So maybe you will enter the literary profession as so many Southern gentlemen and gentlewomen too are doing now and maybe some day you will remember this and write about it. You will be married then I expect and perhaps your wife will want a new gown or a new chair for the house and you can write this and submit it to the magazines. Perhaps you will even remember kindly then the old woman who made you spend a whole afternoon sitting indoors and listening while she talked about people and events you were fortunate enough to escape yourself when you wanted to be out among young friends of your own age."[1]

Though Quentin politely answers "Yessum," he is too wise to accept that explanation of why Miss Rosa has summoned him to her parlor, and he decides that it is not interest in his future literary welfare, but the compulsion to relate certain past events to one who may some day be able to record them, that is behind the old woman's action. Later he realizes that neither is this the reason for Miss Rosa's tale-telling; the truth is that she wants him to go with her that night to an old mansion in the nearby woods and what she is telling him is why she must go out there.

Even though we know, from another and earlier novel, that Quentin Compson did not live to become an author, in this novel Quentin serves as Faulkner's authorial persona, and it may possibly cross our minds that the very book we are reading is that which somehow results from what Quentin Compsin is told by the old lady that day, and from what he later comes to think about it. So far as the purposes of the telling of this story are concerned, Quentin does indeed speak and think as the persona of William Faulkner at that moment—and in another sense, not only for Faulkner but for every other southern author of William Faulkner's time. The task that Quentin undertakes is articulated by him later on, up at Harvard as he and a Canadian friend thrash out the story of the man called Thomas Sutpen. *"Tell about the South, What's it like there. What do they do there. Why do they live there. Why do they live at all."*[2] There are no interrogation marks at the end of those sentences, only periods, for the obligation is assumed on Quentin's part; it is as much self-imposed as given from without, for the injunction to tell about the South is as much the writer's compulsion as the listener's request. The southern author must, indeed, "tell about the South." He has been doing it for 150 years. He is still doing it today.

I want to examine this self-imposed obligation, this compulsion, if you will, on the part of the southern-born writer to be a *southern* writer. I should like to hypothesize, that is, about the "southernness" of the southern writer—what is involved in it, why it has existed and still exists, and what I think it signifies about the South and about its books. The extent to which this consciousness of literary role exists in southern literature can be seen in a comment that one twentieth-century southern novelist has made about another. Here is Robert Penn Warren on the subject of William Faulkner: "James Joyce went forth from Ireland to forge, as he put it, in the words of his hero Stephen Dedalus, the conscience of his race. Faulkner did a more difficult thing. To forge the conscience of his race, he stayed in his native spot and, in his soul, in vice and in virtue, re-enacted the history of that race."[3] Such, as I see it, has been the formidable obligation of the writer in the South.

If you ask him about it, to be sure, he is likely to deny it. This is understandable. William Styron, for example, queried as to whether his first novel was "southern," replied that he did not "consider myself in the southern school, whatever that is. *Lie Down in Darkness*, or most of it, was set in the South, but I don't care if I never write about the South again, really."[4] But Styron did "choose" to write about the South again, and anyone who has read his account of how the subject of the Nat Turner insurrection came to possess his imagination will not be misled by any effort on Styron's part to pretend that as an author he has not felt a strong compulsion to "tell about the South."[5] Long before Styron, Samuel L. Clemens spent much time and effort not only insisting upon his entire emancipation from his southern origins, but proclaiming his vigorous disapproval of southern romanticism and southern rodomontade. But his greatest art is either directly or obliquely focused upon the country along the southern river and the people who lived there when he was young.

For another example, Sidney Lanier may be witnessed, in 1869, deploring "the habit of regarding our literature as *southern* literature, our poetry as *southern* poetry, our pictures as southern pictures. I mean the habit of glossing over the intrinsic defects of artistic productions by appealing to the southern sympathies of the artist's countryman."[6] But notice that pronoun "our": what can it mean? Today, alas, we are likely not only to view Lanier's poetry as southern, but indeed as all too much so. And finally, even Faulkner, despite Quentin Compson's stated sense of obligation, had his moments when he suggested that he was not trying to write about the South, and did not wish to be thought of as doing anything of the kind.* But of course anyone who forms his opinions of what writers are about from what they say in interviews, rather than from what they write in their stories and poems, is very naive. A writer, whether of fiction or poetry, may say what he would like to believe is so, but he writes what he knows is really so.

One might wonder why it is that so many of the best writers of the South have tried to insist that they are not, in any important sense, "southern" writers. For answer, we have to consider what the identification has too often been made to signify. In the year 1907 there was produced the first of a multi-volumed series of books, entitled *The Library of Southern Literature*. Before it was done the set ran on to seventeen volumes in all, gilded and stamped in

---

*As witness the following exchange at the University of Virginia:

Q. "Sir, to what extent were you trying to picture the South and southern civilization as a whole, rather than just Mississippi—or were you?"

A. "Not at all. I was trying to talk about people, using the only tool I knew, which was the country that I knew. No, I wasn't trying to—wasn't writing sociology at all. I was just trying to write about people, which to me are, the important thing. Just the human heart, it's not ideas. I don't know anything about ideas, don't have much confidence in them."[7]

gold. Putting the series together was, the editors declared, a "labor of love and patriotism,"[8] and presumably buying them was expected to be the same. The selections included were designed to exhibit the South's burgeoning literary productivity, and the implication clearly was that any region which could produce so formidable a display of literature was a worthy region indeed.

The numerous volumes of the *Library of Southern Literature* offered the patriotic southerner the privilege of owning selections from the works of a staggering array of authors. The first volume, for example, exhibits representative selections from the writings of, among others, such noted authors as Thomas Albert Smith Adams, Hew Ainslie, Isaac Edwin Emery, Waitman Barbe, Amelia Barr, James Newton Baskett, Kemp Plummer Battle, Frances Courtenay Baylor, and John Henry Boner. Each author's section was preceded by a laudatory biographical sketch.

Lest anyone may have forgotten the work of John Henry Boner, for example, let me quote from the second stanza of his memorable lyric entitled "The Wanderer Back Home":

> From coast to mountain heights
> Old North Carolina lies,
> A cornucopia of delights
> Under her summer skies,
> And autumn gives rich treasure
> To the overflowing horn,
> Adding a juicy measure
> Of grape and rye and corn.[9]

With due allowance for shifts in literary fashion from that day until this, I doubt that there can ever have been a time when that sort of poem was considered worthy of anthologizing for its literary merits alone. Obviously a set of books offering such verse as exemplary of the South's literary achievement was compiled in accordance with standards involving other criteria than literary excellence.

So it is small wonder that, if work of that quality is to be displayed as representative of southern literary taste and literary achievement, then any southern author of genuine talent will not likely be eager to receive a similar accolade. The history of southern literature, in short, has more often than not constituted an effort to extol the third-rate because it is southern, and we can understand why an author of first-rate talent will be uneasy at being told that he too is a southern author, just like John Henry Boner and Waitman Barbe. Edwin A. Alderman and Joel Chandler Harris (or if not they, those who used their names and their authority) apparently saw no incongruity in placing the writings of numerous authors of the order of Hew Ainslie, Waitman Barbe, and John Henry Boner alongside the work of Poe, Simms, Cable, Lanier, and Longstreet. All were southerners, all were authors, so in the view of the editors all belonged within the covers of an anthologized set of volumes designed to prove, in the words of the editors, "that the literary barrenness of the South has been overstated, and its contributions to American letters undervalued, both as to quantity and quality."[10]

There is yet another dimension to it. In the first volume of the *Library of Southern Literature,* along with the work of the poets and the storytellers, may be found selections from the writings of Judah P. Benjamin, Thomas H. Benton, and Albert Taylor Bledsoe. The first two were United States senators, from Louisiana and Missouri, respectively, and Benjamin was also a noted member of Jefferson Davis's cabinet. As for Bledsoe, he was the famed apologist for the Confederacy, author of *Is Davis a Traitor?,* the polemicist to whom no less a person than General Robert E. Lee is reported to have remarked, after the war, "Doctor, you must take care of yourself; you have a great work to do; we all look to you for our vindication."[11] These men were not

litterateurs; they were politicians and political pamphle-
teers. Equally clearly, in the eyes of the editors of the
Library of Southern Literature, they too were southern
writers, and the abundant presence of political polemic in
a series designed to display the literary harvest of the southern states exemplifies the close relationship between
politics and literature in the imagination of the nineteenth-century South. New England authors, of course, also
concerned themselves with politics. We are familiar with
the "Biglow Papers," with Emerson's "Ode" to Channing,
Thoreau's "Civil Disobedience," Whittier's "Massachusetts to Virginia," and so on. But where in New England
literature could be political, in the Old South and thereafter, straight political writing was considered to be literature.

So much, then, for the *Library of Southern Literature.*
Most of us have heard the old joke about the delegates to
the Savannah Convention of 1856 resolving that there be
created a southern literature, and then resolving that the
Hon. William Gilmore Simms, LL.D., be requested to
write it. (It is not true, according to Simm's biographer: in
fact, what happened was that Simms was slighted by not
being asked to take part, and among those chosen to super-
vise the textbooks for a truly patriotic southern literature
was Bledsoe, which is even more to my point.[12]) The record does show, however, that when in 1847 the poet James
Mathewes Legaré was writing around to secure support for
a projected southern literary magazine, he addressed a letter to John C. Calhoun, enclosing a prospectus. Calhoun
not only sent in his subscription, but replied that "we
want, above all other things, a southern literature, from
school books up to works of the highest order."[13]* We may
be sure that if Legaré had been enabled to found his liter-

---

* There is an old Charleston pleasantry to the effect that Calhoun was
the only man ever to have written a love poem beginning with the word
"whereas."

ary magazine, any material published in it would have been properly orthodox on the subject of slavery and states rights. This was only natural. There is no reason to think that Legaré would have wished it otherwise. What is clear is that both before and after the Civil War, and on into the 1900s, a political purity was expected of the southern writer that kept him from questioning the social values of his community. That the orthodoxy was willingly assumed does not matter; indeed the very fact that the nineteenth-century southern writer did not sense any contradiction between his literary goals and his social views is all the more significant here. As Allen Tate pointed out, ante-bellum southern society "was hag-ridden with politics," for the South had aristocratic rule, and "all aristocracies are obsessed politically," so that "the best intellectual energy goes into politics and goes of necessity."[14] In the postbellum South it was hardly very different. The planter aristocracy was no longer dominant, but now the defeat of the war and the hardships of the Reconstruction had enforced upon the region a new orthodoxy on the subject of race relations that equally did not countenance dissent. The only two southern authors of the century who seriously challenged the social arrangements of their native region were Clemens and Cable, the former doing so from Hartford, Connecticut, and the latter pulling up stakes in New Orleans almost immediately after first speaking out and removing to New England himself.

The typical antebellum nineteenth-century southern writer, then, was no political or social iconoclast. He wrote his stories and poems to be read by the home folks. That they often were not so read was not his fault; certainly he constructed them so as not to give offense. He did not think it his duty to criticize the political and social views of his fellow southerners, for in general they were his own views as well. As a member of the southern community he wore his literary identity gracefully, as befitted a gentleman of the community who was a writer; the literature that he produced, alas, reflects it. So we should not be surprised that in a later day, when no such political and social consensus existed, the popular assumption that a southern writer must share the characteristic southern views on race and other matters might be enough to make writers of independent opinions uncomfortable at being identified as southern writers.

Recurringly we come upon the more serious nineteenth-century southern author's occasional uneasiness with this community arrangement. Here, for example, is William Gilmore Simms on the South's preoccupation with politics to the exclusion of imaginative literature: "No periodical can well succeed in the South, which does not include the *political* constituent. The mind of the South is active chiefly in the direction of politics. . . . The only reading people in the South are those to whom politics is the bread of life."[15] Here is the *Southern Literary Messenger* in 1856, deploring the South's unwillingness to allow its writers to criticize their homeland: "There is a foolish soreness in our southern fancies about having any blur or blemish pointed out in our society, which is absolutely childish. There is a certain class of minds who see in every effort of the kind, some imaginary thrust at the 'peculiar institution.' "[16] Here is Henry Timrod on the South's abiding taste for literary mediocrity: "There is scarcely a city of any size in the South which has not its clique of amateur critics, poets and philosophers, the regular business of whom is to demonstrate truisms, settle questions which nobody else would think of discussing, to confirm themselves in opinions which have been picked up from the rubbish of seventy years agone, and able all to persuade each other that together they constitute a society not much inferior to that in which figured Burke and Johnson, Goldsmith and

Sir Joshua. All of these being oracles, they are unwilling
to acknowledge the claims of a professional writer, lest in
so doing they should disparage their own authority."[17]

After the war we find George W. Cable, addressing the
commencement exercises at the University of Louisiana,
asking his audience whether the South shall continue to
demand of a new writer "that he shall bow down to our
crochets and whims? . . . Will he not be expected to practice certain amiable and cowardly oversights and silences
in order to smooth the frown of sections or parties and
pacify the autocratic voice of ruling classes or established
ideas?" "The writers of the South," he pleaded, "must be
free." Southerners must be willing to "throw our society,
or section, our institutions, ourselves, wide open to their
criticism and correction, reserving the right to resent only
what we can refute."[18]

Finally here is Joel Chandler Harris objecting, "Does a
publisher fill a paper full of trash from the composition
books of romantic school-girls? We must all applaud and
buy for the benefit of southern literature. Does Miss
Sweetie Wildwood get together a lot of sickening doggerel?
The newspapers must gush over the gush, not only for the
purpose of building up southern literature but because
Miss Sweetie is a daughter of Colonel Wildwood. What is
the result? Why, simply this, that the stuff we are in the
habit of calling southern literature is not only a burlesque
upon true literary art, but a humiliation and a disgrace to
the people whose culture it is supposed to represent."[19]

That is what they said. The sincerity of the lamentation
is not to be questioned. Yet when we examine the careers
of these writers, what is striking is that, with the notable
exception of Cable, the occasional protests they recorded
about the obsessiveness of politics, the mediocrity of taste,
and the hypersensitivity to criticism were only that: occasional protests. That is to say, they complained, and then

kept right on living and writing in the South. Take, for example, Simms. At times of disappointment and despair we find him deploring the fact that he had not gone North and pursued fame and fortune, and sometimes threatening to do so even yet. But though he traveled to New York regularly to see his editors and his literary friends there, he always returned home. And despite his protests over the way in which the southern reading audience was obsessed with politics, a look at his correspondence will show that he too was very political-minded. Not only did he hold office himself for a time, but politicians such as James Henry Hammond, William Porcher Miles, and others were among his closest correspondents. He began his career as a political journalist, and at least until after the close of the Civil War there was almost no period in his career in which he was not involved in strongly articulating a political position; indeed there were periods when he seemed so obsessed with politics that there was little time left for literature. The notion that he might go up to New York and become a man of letters pure and simple may have seemed appealing to him at times, but not to the extent that he ever acted upon it.

Or consider the case of Joel Chandler Harris. The editorial from which I quoted, in which he complains about the confusion of southern patriotic effusion with southern literature, was after all published in a newspaper, the *Atlanta Constitution*. Across the desk from Harris sat his friend Henry W. Grady, entrepreneur, journalist, promoter of the New South. No newspaper was ever more assiduous in advancing the claims of things southern than the *Constitution* under Grady. The *Constitution* was the South's foremost propagandist for everything—business, agriculture, literature, racial segregation. There is little reason to believe that Harris ever consciously dissented, during Grady's lifetime at any rate, from the promotional

policies of his friend. It is difficult, therefore, to see Joel
Chandler Harris as indignant foe to the southern pro-
pensity for self-congratulation, and it should be remembered that the *Library of Southern Literature,* which bore
his name as coeditor, is crowded with specimens of the Miss
Sweetie Wildwood variety of southern literature. If Harris
did little except lend his name to the venture, nothing
indicates that he objected to its policy of patriotic in-
clusiveness.

With only the merest handful of exceptions, then, southern writers who felt at times that the South was no place
for a writer nonetheless remained there by choice, and did
not seek importantly to dissociate themselves from the public attitudes of the community in which they resided. One
thinks, by contrast, of the long procession of Irish authors
who, born like the southerner into a largely rural society
and removed from the literary center by the Irish Sea, set
forth to London to live as writers. Ireland, to be sure, was
a conquered province, while until the Civil War the South
was no such thing, but something there seems to have been
that kept the southerners home, for all their occasional
despair at the southern literary prospect, and that did not,
under remarkably similar circumstances, keep the young
Irish writers home.

One can hardly claim that they stayed in the South because the Man of Letters occupied any kind of exalted
position. James Branch Cabell delighted in quoting a passage from an address of welcome to Charles Dickens by
Thomas Ritchie of the Richmond *Enquirer,* when the
British novelist visited Virginia in 1842. Editor Ritchie
explained to the distinguished guest that "the *forte* of the
Old Dominion is to be found in the masculine production
of her statesmen, her Washington, her Jefferson, and her
Madison, who," the editor said, "have never indulged in
works of imagination, in the charms of romance, or in the

mere beauties of the *belles lettres.*" Cabell remarks that "the exact trick of it, one notes, lies in that 'mere.' "[20] Cabell's view of the antebellum attitude is corroborated again and again by contemporary sources. We all know the story of how Lord Morpeth visited Charleston, asked for Simms, and was told that Simms was not considered such a great man in Charleston. "Simms not a great man! Then for God's sake, who is your great man?" the Englishman responded.[21] Well might Simms's friend Paul Hamilton Hayne, writing to him in 1859, lament the lot of the serious writer in "this material, debased, provincial, narrowminded South" and assure his friend that "prosperity, praise, 'troops of friends,' and admirers" would have been the novelist's lot "had you removed at an early age to Massachusetts or Europe."[22] This is exactly what Simms thought, at times anyway. All that he had accomplished, he wrote once, "has been poured to waste in Charleston, which has never smiled on any of my labors, which has steadily ignored my claims, which has disparaged me to the last, has been the last place to give me its adhesion, to which I owe no favor, having never received an office, or a compliment, or a dollar at her hands." And he asks, rhetorically, "Great God! what is the sort of slavery which brings me hither!"[23]* Yet he did not go North.

The obvious explanation for the near-unanimous refusal of the nineteenth-century southern author to pursue fame and fortune elsewhere is, of course, patriotism. Hayne assures Simms that at least his friend possesses "the consciousness of having been true to the Penates, of having illustrated, as none other has, the *genius loci,* under disadvantages which would have sunk a weaker mind and corrupted a less manly and heroic heart."[24] Patriotism

---

* In strict justice it ought to be noted that toward the end of Simms's life Charleston did seek to amend its earlier neglect with several notable acts of appreciation and recognition.

there was indeed. But patriotism is not an abstract emotion.
It is a loyalty to a particular place, in a particular time,
that is involved. These men were *southern* patriots, and it
is to the nineteenth-century South and its society that we
must look if we are to understand what it was that kept
them tied so securely to their homeland. We must try,
therefore, to conceive of the Old South as it appeared to
its writers.

Now this is a very difficult thing for us to do. Looking
at the past without imposing our own moral and social
attitudes upon it is always a chancy affair, but when it is
the past of the South that is involved, it becomes especially
risky. For the modern reader there is laid over the picture
of the Old South an enormous screen that must inevitably
distort our view of it. That screen is slavery. The Old South
—the South of Simms, Timrod, and Poe—believed in the
moral right to own human beings as property, if they were
black. And the post–Civil War South—the South of Harris and Page and Cable—believed with almost complete
unanimity in the total inferiority of the black man, to the
degree that it placed him in a state of virtual peonage.
Much of the history of the twentieth-century South has
revolved about the painful liberation from those beliefs,
and we are still so deeply involved in the transaction that
we find it almost impossible to look at the South's past
without seeing it and judging it in those terms. We confront the fact that William Gilmore Simms, who was no
Whig but an ardent Jacksonian Democrat and a spokesman for the Young America movement, not only believed
in human slavery and owned slaves, but was so enthusiastic
a defender of the system that several years before the war he
went North to lecture in public on the benevolence of the
institution. His view was shared by almost all the antebellum southern writers. And in the post-Reconstruction
South almost every southern author except Clemens and

Cable believed in the inherent and total inferiority of black people. All this is not a matter for debate; it is on the record. And knowing it, we find it very difficult to sympathize with much that those who held such views said and thought and wrote.

And yet we must try. For however we may feel about the matter ourselves, we cannot see the South as its antebellum authors saw it if we take the position that because slavery was immoral, therefore the writers of the Old South were either savages or else hypocrites when they declared that it was not. Much though we might like to believe otherwise, they were not dissembling when they defended slavery. The abundant evidence is that the southern man of letters was not morally uncomfortable in his advocacy of slavery, and did not writhe unduly in the confines of an ideology that placed him in the position of having to defend it. What is even more difficult to realize, perhaps, is that he did not spend very much time either desperately trying to avoid the subject or else trying to invent equally desperate rationales for defending it. He mostly accepted it, and if sometimes its ramifications disturbed him, he was convinced that the problem did not admit of a solution in the near future. Besides there were other things that seemed more important to be thinking about.

Did this make him a moral leper? If we decree that it must, we are guilty, I fear, of considerable smugness. Have we not, in our own time, also found difficulty in accepting the evidence of our eyes on various matters involving race and war and other topics, when our self-interest, real or apparent, has suggested otherwise? Does this make us all criminals, or only painfully fallible human beings? If the latter, then knowing what we do about the history of slavery and racial ideology in the western world, we might be more careful before we casually condemn the nineteenth-century South as a den of moral renegades.

I say all this not in an attempt to make excuses either for slavery or for the writers of the Old South, but because it seems to me worthwhile to try to understand them. Likewise it seems to me that a great deal of the study of the nineteenth-century South done during the past quarter-century or so has been conducted on premises that make it very difficult to understand the time or the place in question. We have, for example, conducted exhaustive analyses of what nineteenth-century southerners have written, both in fiction and poetry and in their nonfiction, their correspondence, their journals, and so on, eagerly searching for evidence, between the lines as it were, that in their heart of hearts they disapproved of slavery and secretly believed in the dignity of all men black and white. And we have found such evidence, too. I myself have pointed out, for example, that Simms, even while cheerfully advocating slavery, wrote a novel in which the very premises of slavery and even racism are thoroughly negated, so that he found it necessary to wrench his story back into the proper ideology at the close.[25] But in so saying, we focus upon a moral contretemps which did not seem nearly so important to Simms as it does to us. For Simms it was not an important logical contradiction, and neither was it for Simms's readers. So if we concentrate our inquiry into Simms and his time and place upon the existence of such things, we will not be importantly enabling ourselves to understand either the writer or his times.

Many students of the Old South have painstakingly scrutinized what nineteenth-century southerners wrote, with the idea of discovering therein an underlying sense of moral guilt over slavery and a defiant attempt to palliate or mask that guilt. The truth is that for the most part the guilt is simply not there. The antebellum novelist's failure to deal realistically with his society has been attributed to slavery and to the secret suspicion on his part that if once he began examining society's social premises, he would have to confront his own moral dilemma. Doubtless the superficiality of nineteenth-century southern literature in respect to social analysis is in important ways due to the presence of slavery in the values of the society. But it is a complex matter, and we will go wrong if we attribute to the antebellum writer any conscious turning away from social criticism because of pressures brought to bear on him by his neighbors. *He* did not think along such lines most of the time. That was simply not what he thought that literature was supposed to do.

How could the southern author possibly have believed in the moral good of so inhuman an institution as slavery? From our vantage point in time we find that incredible. Yet he *did* believe in it. He believed that slavery was a benevolent institution, though sometimes abused, sanctioned by Holy Writ and justifiable by the nature of the African, and in any case infinitely more merciful than the impersonal wage slavery of English and northern capitalism. When slavery was attacked he was indignant. He knew better: there was the irrefutable evidence of his own eyes. Were not most slaves generally cheerful, happy? Were not their relations with the masters more often than not intimate and affectionate? Were not many slaves all but members of the planter's family? Did they not sing at their work? Were not the aged and infirm given food and shelter after their working days were done? Were not the slaves far better off on southern plantations than as ignorant savages in the African jungle? If only those who criticized the "peculiar institution" from afar, on grounds of abstract morality, would come down and see for themselves what a fine thing it was, they would then cease to pay attention to the fanatical Abolitionists and their inflammatory defamations and lies. Certainly there were abuses and cruelties on some plantations, he would grant, but these were vastly

in the minority. After all, why would a slaveowner pur-
posely cripple the capacity of a valuable slave to do a full
day's work? "As for our 'infernal institution,' as you mildly
call it," wrote Paul Hamilton Hayne to his friend Richard
Henry Stoddard in 1856, "we will discuss *that question,*
my dear Richard, when I shall have the honor (as I hope
to have some day) of entertaining Mrs. S. & yourself under
my humble roof-tree in Carolina, with said 'infernal institution' right under our eyes—I fear that the argument, if
attempted between us in our present relations would simply be a *geographical,* not a *political* discussion."[26]

Hayne was a slaveholder. He knew many other slaveholders. He was satisfied that African slavery was, in an
imperfect world, a benevolent, humane arrangement, and
he was sure that if only his northern friend could see it as
it actually existed, instead of as depicted in antislavery
propaganda, he too would be convinced. Today, when the
nature of the South's "peculiar institution" has been sub-
jected to stringent analysis, the fashion is to think of it as
utterly without redeeming qualities, and therefore to view
all who sought to defend it as hypocrites or knaves. Yet if
we read the correspondence of Simms, or Hayne, or others
like them, we must surely come away with the conviction
that these were good men, kind men, honest men, who
wanted to do what was right and good.

The slave system in the Old South has come to be depicted as an unremitting hell on earth for the black man.
It has been likened to the concentration camp of the World
War II period, with the implied corollary that the slaveholders were no better than Nazis, in effect. At the risk of
appearing to try to justify slavery, I can only say that I
cannot believe that it was so. I cannot believe it if for no
other reason than that too many good men, men who were
kind and honest and well-intentioned, men like Simms and
Hayne and many others, were able in good conscience to

live within it. It is undeniable that they were blind to its essential inhumanity, in that they did not recognize that for any man to be owned by another man was unacceptable as a way of life for the one who is owned. That their inability to perceive the outraged human dignity of a man owned as property was a severe limitation on their moral perspective also goes without question. But at the same time these men, and many others like them, were perfectly well able to recognize physical cruelty and viciousness and barbarity when they saw them, and the uncritical belief they held in the benevolent nature of African slavery could not have been held by them if slavery had been in daily practice the unrelieved debauchery and entire horror that many present-day scholars seem to be convinced that it was. The concentration camp comparison undoubtedly has its psychological usefulness, but before we accept it uncritically, it might be well to consider certain points of fact. The Nazi concentration camps of the 1930s and 1940s were places where millions of men, women, and children were put to death. The number of survivors was pitifully small. By contrast it has been established that no more than about 427,000 slaves were imported into the United States in all, yet by 1810 their numbers had increased to one million, and by 1860 to about four million. In other words there were ten times the number of Negro slaves in the United States on the eve of the Civil War as there were slaves imported into the country from Africa. What kind of concentration camp was it in which the inhabitants managed to multiply in numbers by almost 1000 percent?[27]*

I am certainly not defending the justice of slavery, either

---

* If it be objected that the tenfold increase in the slave population was due only to the financial profit that slave-owners would make through breeding them like animals, the census figures also show that during the four decades following the end of slavery, when no such incentives existed, the ratio of increase of black to white Americans maintained precisely the same balance as during the prewar decades![28]

in theory or practice. It is, quite simply, indefensible. What I am insisting upon, however, is the essential humanity of most of the slaveholders—not *as* slaveholders, but as men. For I cannot ignore the evidence that, then as now, most white southerners were no worse and no better than human beings everywhere, and that however much they were involved in the maintenance of an inhumane institution, in actual practice they must have brought to that institution the same kind of individual decency and kindness that they brought to everything else they did. This is not to contend, as the proslavery apologists would have it, that the slaves enjoyed being slaves, and did not object to being enslaved. It is only to maintain that, given the essential barbarity of human ownership, men of good will could and did, through fundamental kindness and fairness, render even slavery tolerable.

For the relationship of master and slave was, after all, a relationship between human beings, and if exposed to the baser possibilities of human nature, was also open to the more ennobling instincts. Here the Marxist historian Eugene Genovese in instructive, I think. Insisting that slavery in the antebellum South was basically precapitalistic and feudal in nature, and not an agricultural version of nine-teenth-century American capitalism, Genovese stresses the necessary interdependence of master and slave, in which each profoundly affected the other. "The slave," he writes, "stood interposed between his master and the object his master desired (that which was produced); thus, the mas-ter related to the subject only mediately, through the slave. The slaveholder commanded the products of another's labor, but by the same process was forced into dependence upon this other."[29] And Genovese maintains that "the planters commanded southern politics and set the tone of social life. Theirs was an aristocratic, antibourgeois spirit with values and mores emphasizing family and status, a strong code of honor, and aspirations to luxury, ease, and accomplishment. In the planters' community, paternalism provided the standard of human relationships, and politics and statecraft were the duties and responsibilities of gentlemen."[30] In such a relationship, however disadvantageous the slave's position was, he was not an instrument of production but an individual, and the dependence of the slaveholder on the slave was direct and open. Thus Genovese insists that both master and slave affected each other profoundly, and the human relationship that was theirs was essentially different from that between manufacturer and worker, since it was not disguised and hidden by the process of the exchange of commodities in the marketplace.[31] The slave was not merely a means to an end; he was on the scene for good, and the relationship between slaves and master was between individuals and, both for better and for worse, humanly direct and personal.

To be sure, this is no answer to the question that Mrs. Stowe propounded in the concluding remarks to *Uncle Tom's Cabin:* "Is *man* ever a creature to be trusted with wholly irresponsible power?"[32] Nor is it an answer to the fact of the auction block, or to the memoirs of Frederick Douglass, or to the Nat Turner insurrection. But it does help to explain, at least, how it was that the antislavery journalist and poet William Cullen Bryant, after a visit to William Gilmore Simms's plantation, could write the following description of what he had seen: "The blacks of this region are a cheerful, careless, dirty race, not hard-worked, and in many respects indulgently treated. It is, of course, the desire of the master that his slaves shall work hard; on the other hand, the determination of the slave is to lead as easy a life as he can. The master has power of punishment on his side; the slave, on his, an invincible indolence, and a thousand expedients learned by long practice. The result is a compromise, in which each party yields something, and a good-natured though imperfect and slovenly obedience on one side is purchased by good treatment on the other."[33]

I have made this too long, and I fear rather peripheral, digression into the nature of the slave society of the Old South because I want to try to characterize the relationship of the southern writer to his community, as I see it, and it does not seem likely that we can properly grasp the peculiarly intense hold that the southern community exerted over the southern writer unless we try to see slavery as it looked to his eyes. The loyalty of the writer to the community was such that it could hold him there despite conditions that were notably disadvantageous for writers. We have to ask, therefore, what were the compensating advantages that negated the drawbacks. What, in short, was so attractive about living in the South that made its writers not only accept but proudly extoll and defend a society which practiced slavery?

The way of life of the Old South has been the subject of so much investigation, and also of so much mythologizing and demythologizing, that one scarcely dares generalize about it for fear of unwittingly taking part in the folklore, or else of failing to take account of the facts. We are concerned, however, not with the Old South as it was, but with why its writers clung to it so closely. One way to get at the matter, therefore, might be to look at precisely those shortcomings that posterity has pronounced (and in general justifiably) upon the work of the writers in question, and also upon the strictures they themselves uttered concerning their situations, the appropriateness of which we have no reason to doubt. We might summarize the indictment this way:

(1) The literature is superficial, failing to go below the surfaces of the society into an exploration of its underlying problems.

(2) Because the writers rose so vigorously to the defense of slavery, the literature suffers from the moral blindness therein involved. (Cf. Timrod's "The Cotton Boll.")

(3) There was an inability on the part of southern readers to distinguish between important literary effort and local amateur productions, which resulted in much attention paid to mediocrity and an insufficiency of attention to the few really important writers.

(4) The Old South expected its authors to perform political roles as propagandists, and the intellectual life of the community was so dominated by politics that artistic interests were relatively unimportant.

What it seems to come down to, I think, is that there is a failure on the part of the nineteenth-century southern writer to be detached from his community. He was too much a part of it, too willing to accept its values, too reluctant to throw its flaws and blemishes into literary image. The community itself would not give him special treatment; it judged his work by its own community standards, and insisted that his work perform community duties. Compare Hawthorne's dissection of New England and its past, in love and in anger, with Simms's woodenly patriotic romances of the southern past, and the superior detachment and objectivity of perception on the part of the New England author is obvious.

But let us, for the purposes of argument, turn this objection around. The fact that the southern writer was insufficiently detached from the attitudes of his community carries with it a corollary proposition: that there *was* a community of which he could be part. His very acceptance of its values, his eager involvement in its politics, his willingness to defend its "peculiar institution"—all testify to the existence of such a community, and to the place he held within it. He belonged.

He appears to have possessed, both in antebellum times

and for decades thereafter, membership in such a community, and to have been able to define his human identity, to his own satisfaction at least, in terms of it. The same Simms who could remark so bleakly on Charleston's refusal to recognize his claims could also declare, to a Yankee *litterateur* come down to see how the South had benefitted from losing the Civil War, that "Charleston, sir, was the finest city in the world; not a large city, but the finest. South Carolina, sir, was the flower of modern civilization. Our people were the most hospitable, the most accomplished, having the highest degree of culture and the highest sense of honor, of any people, I will not say of America, sir, but of any country on the globe. And they are so still, even in their temporary destitution."[34] Allowing for the likelihood that John T. Trowbridge would seem to have aroused Simms's latent outrage over the results of the just-completed conflict, it is still obvious that the novelist was deeply attached to his native city, and that resentment over patrician neglect of his merits did not finally weaken that attachment.

We will find a similar attachment on the part of almost all the nineteenth-century southern writers. There must, therefore, have been very real compensations in the community identity to make up for the South's inadequacies as a literary marketplace and its relative indifference to the "mere beauties" of the belles lettres, and if we will approach the matter from the standpoint not of why the southern author failed to muster the detachment needed for important art, but of why he was so devoted to his society that he could not and would not view it critically, we can see some of the attractions in the very inadequacies themselves.

Consider Timrod's lament, already quoted, that the South of his day was so filled with "amateur critics, poets and philosophers, the regular business of whom is to demonstrate truisms," and to "persuade each other that they constitute a society not inferior" to that of eighteenth-century England. These amateurs, Timrod complains, are "unwilling to acknowledge the claims of a professional writer." Doubtless he had Charleston, and in particular William J. Grayson, in mind when he composed that indictment. But what is he saying? That in a community such as antebellum Charleston, insufficient distinction was made between amateur and professional author, which is to say that the professional writer was not held by his fellow townsmen to be a separate kind of citizen, to be considered as existing outside the everyday life of that community. We have seen from the *Library of Southern Literature* that this attitude resulted in the praising of a great deal of mediocre writing, but it also reflected the attitude of a community of which the writer, as citizen, is an organic member, and not a harmless freak. Paul Hamilton Hayne tells of how, as a boy, he attended a political rally in which the cry rose for "Simms, Gilmore Simms," whereupon the novelist came forth "with a slow, stately step under the full blaze of the chandeliers, a man in the prime of life, tall, vigorous, and symmetrically formed," to harangue his audience on topics related to the Mexican War.[35] If this incident represents, as it did for Simms's biographer William Peterfield Trent, another example of the sad dispersal of Simms's literary talents by the South's obsession with politics, it also offers us a picture of a man who is in close involvement with the main concerns of his community, and possesses a public role within that community's scheme of things.

Was Simms an exception in this respect? Only to a degree (in one sense, Simms is *always* an exception). Go down the list of the leading nineteenth-century southern authors, and one is impressed by the extent to which most of them played active public roles in their society. They

edited newspapers, practiced law, held office, served in the
professions. It is said, and with reason, that a writer could
not earn a living *as a writer* in the Old South. This is quite
true. But the corollary is that the literary man of the nineteenth-century South was engaged in the everyday life of
his community, economic, social, political, cultural. Such
reality as he knew and craved was to be found within the
community. That his art would have been more memorable had he felt the need to retreat to a Walden Pond* or
to an Old Manse is very likely; but he did not. He seems
to have felt no urge to go off and found Brook Farms. Antebellum southern life is remarkable for the almost total absence of any of the utopian colonies that were otherwise so
much a part of American life during the period when
industrialism was making its presence markedly felt for
the first time. The southern writer was familiar with fields
and streams, and he wrote often of the attractions of nature,
but the idea that by abandoning his community for a cabin
in the wilds he would be better able to front life in its
essentials was apparently not for him.

It is certainly not my objective here—I am not so naive
as that—to try to determine just why antebellum society
was able to offer the southern writer so organic a role as I
have sketched, for that would involve settling the matter of
what that society was and was not, a task that better men
than myself have essayed at great length and with varying
conclusions. I shall content myself with a few generalizations. Whether because or in spite of the presence within
it of African slavery (one suspects that both are somehow

---

* One might consider the difference between Thoreau's masterpiece
and that best known of nineteenth-century southern accounts of life in the
wilds, William Elliott's *Carolina Sports by Land and Water* (1846), a
book which Thoreau admired, though with reservations about Elliott's
inconsistencies. Elliott is a plantation owner who pursued his fish and
game with his slaves at his side and with gentlemen to share in the sport.
His book remains a set of delightful hunting and fishing stories. Thoreau's
is a searching critique of the values of his society. There is nothing like
Walden in all of southern literature before *I'll Take My Stand*.

involved) , the society of the Old South was given to a devotion to leisure, which some have called laziness or hedon-
ism, and others have called freedom from materialism. The
Old South placed a less than Calvinistic importance upon
the Work Ethic. The whites tended to feel that too much
work was degrading, while the blacks were opposed to it
because the fruits of their labor generally went to someone
else. Southern society tended to cultivate the amenities. It
placed considerable emphasis on manners, believed in
noblesse oblige, cultivated the paternalistic concept of role.
Consumption, and the display of consumption, was more
important than acquisition, for as Genovese and others
have pointed out, the Old South was precapitalistic and
even feudal, and its symbols of aristocratic distinction were
land and slaves, not money. At their best, says Genovese,
"Southern ideals constituted a rejection of the crass, vulgar,
inhumane elements of capitalist society. The slaveholders
simply could not accept the idea that the cash nexus offered
a permissible basis for human relations. Even the vulgar
parvenu of the Southwest embraced the plantation myth
and refused to make a virtue of necessity by glorifying
the competitive side of slavery as civilization's highest
achievement."[36] What the Old South aspired to was expressed by Henry Timrod in imagery that emphasizes the
notion of leisure and gentility:

>   ... the type
> Whereby we shall be known in every land
> Is that vast gulf which laves our Southern strand,
> And through the cold, untempered ocean pours
> Its genial streams, that far off Arctic shores
> May sometimes catch upon the softened breeze
> Strange tropic warmth and hints of summer seas![37]

Because it was a society imbued with the consciousness
of role, such attention was given to the social arts. Southerners might slight the local literary magazines, for ex-

ample, but they thronged to the theatre. In their social life they played at being gentlemen of leisure. The fascination that the romances of Walter Scott seem to have held for them, and which Mark Twain so deplored, arose from the ideals of chivalry and manners that Scott sometimes emphasized. That the southerners took this seriously is evident, for example, in that way that during the war, in the midst of some of the most bloody and unromantic fighting, they seemed, to judge from their diaries and letters, to have thought of each other in terms of the border chivalry. In the Old South the social role was paramount. In C. Vann Woodward's words "it is possible that a majority of the players identified themselves completely with their roles as 'real life'—as completely perhaps as the saints, prophets and come-outers in other quarters found identity in their roles. At least the cast for the Old South drama, slaves included, often acted as if they did, and sometimes they put on rather magnificent performances."[38]

Within this system of communal role-playing the southern writer seems to have enjoyed a modest but secure part, and the performance apparently made it possible for him to define himself as a man by his conduct within it. He was able, in short, to maintain in a small way the kind of full participation as a man within his community which Emerson, in his American Scholar address, declared was being destroyed by the specialization that an urbanizing, industrializing America was demanding of its citizens. He was not Novelist, Poet; he was Man of Letters who wrote novels, poems.

We ought not, however, attempt to make too much of this, for however enviable that so-called "organic society" may seem in theory, we cannot forget that there were, within the nineteenth-century southern version of it, some very severe limitations. Genovese and others have shown the dire condition of its agricultural underpinnings; there is good reason to believe that the Civil War only precipitated what would surely have been a general collapse of its feudal economy within a matter of a few decades. It is impossible to overlook the fact that African slavery lay at the foundations of the society: the gentlemanly ideal was being purchased at a considerable human cost, and when the promissory note became due in the 1860s, the price, along with the accrued interest, proved to be very steep. Indeed we are still paying on the debt today. The basic fragility of the planter-dominated community that was the Old South has been documented by numerous scholars.

Finally, if the hope of every good writer is to create work that will outlast him, we cannot fail to realize that the cost to the nineteenth-century southern author of belonging to a society in which he could be active participant rather than distanced observer was a literature of surfaces, strikingly deficient in the deeper exploration of human identity that great literary art provides. As Allen Tate warns, "The very merits of the Old South tend to confuse the issue: its comparative stability, its realistic limitation of the acquisitive impulse, its preference for human relations compared to relations economic, tempt the historian to defend the poor literature simply because he feels that the old society was a better place to live in than the new. It is a great temptation—if you do not read the literature."[39]

For though we may cherish the ideal of the organic, harmonious society, with the artist not split apart from it and forced into silence, cunning and exile (whether physical or spiritual exile it does not matter), it seems undeniable that, at least from the seventeenth century onward, it has not normally worked that way. The important American writings of the nineteenth century, as well as those of our own day, have been written for the most part by men and women who were distanced from the attitudes and values of the average citizen of their time, and from the kind of literature that he demanded. There is no need here to rehearse the story of the oblique relationship to American society of its greatest artists; suffice it to say that it existed, and that those writers for whom the distance from the popular culture was not so notable are for the most part not the writers whose works have importantly lasted. The fact that the southern writer does not make his spiritual break from the standards of his culture—did not want to or feel it necessary to do it—means for us that most of the literature of the nineteenth-century South is superficial and shallow, designed to appeal to an audience that did not want its own values and its social arrangements held up to critical scrutiny.

Of all the southern authors of the nineteenth century there are only two whose work seems at its best to transcend the limitations of the time and place, and attain the status of major literary achievement. They are Edgar Allan Poe and Samuel L. Clemens, and it is no accident that neither was able to live out his life within the southern community. Both these men went North (Clemens by way of Nevada and California), and the best writings of both exist in a special, and for some a debatable, relationship to what we usually think of as southern literature. Allen Tate wrote of Poe that "it was not John Allan who drove Poe out of Virginia. . . . Allan was for once, the spokesman of Virginia, of the plantation South. There was no place for Poe in the spiritual community of Virginia. . . . It was obvious, even to John Allan, I suppose, that here was no dabbler who would write pleasant, genteel poems and stories for magazines where other dabbling gentlemen printed their pleasant, genteel stories and poems. Anybody could have looked at Poe and known that he meant business."[40] As for Mark Twain, the circumstances that caused him to depart were of a different sort, and I propose to touch upon them in my next lecture. Suffice it to say here that *Huckle-*

berry Finn could not have been written by a man living in
the South during his lifetime, and equally it could not have
been written by a man who had not once lived there.

In the twentieth century, of course, it has been a different
matter. In my final lecture I hope to examine that topic.
For now let me return to Quentin Compson and his self-
assumed burden to "tell about the South." William Faulkner lived for most of his days in Oxford, Mississippi. It was
there that he wrote all his best novels. William Faulkner
was a member of his community. He went on hunting trips
with his friends, and he played golf and attended the Ole
Miss football games, and he wrote letters to the editor of
the newspaper about the liquor laws. He resided in Oxford, he knew most of its older inhabitants, and it was his
home. He very much preferred living there to living in
Hollywood or New York or even Charlottesville. But William Faulkner was not a citizen of Oxford, Mississippi, in
the way that William Gilmore Simms was a citizen of
Charleston, South Carolina. William Faulkner quarreled
deeply with the opinions of most of his fellow citizens on
the most important political and social issues of his day,
and he did not speak for most of Mississippi when he wrote
about such issues. Nor did William Faulkner write his
books for his community to read. All things considered,
he would doubtless have preferred his novels to be more
popular with his neighbors than they were, but there were
other things that mattered more to him, and that led him
to write stories that were read in New York and Paris and
Stockholm more often than in Mississippi. Faulkner's literary life was not something that he could share with most
of his fellow citizens of Oxford. They knew he was a writer,
and after he became famous they stood slightly in awe of
him, but those among them who actually tried reading his
books either did not understand them or, if they did, dis-

approved very strongly of some of the things he said. As
one of his fellow townsmen put it, "Some of Faulkner's
writings are about as popular in his home country as a dead
skunk would be in a sleeping bag."[41] Now of course William Gilmore Simms felt also that his fellow townsmen did
not read his books as often or as enthusiastically as they
ought to, but if they did not, it was not because they were
offended by what was in them. If Simms had won a Nobel
Prize for Literature, it is hardly likely that the leading
newspaper of the capital city of South Carolina would have
carried an editorial deploring the award. Equally one cannot imagine William Faulkner ever editing an equivalent
of *The Charleston Book: a Miscellany in Prose and Verse*
(1845), and remarking in its Advertisement that though
the work included is all by amateurs, "there is a liveliness
of fancy, a fluency of expression, and a general readiness
of resources, indicating such a presence of the imaginative
faculty, as leaves no doubt of the capacity of the community, from which the work is drawn, to engage with great
success in the active pursuits of literature."[42]

Allowing for the individual personalities of Faulkner
and Simms, it seems to me that we can safely say that most
of the antebellum southern writers enjoyed pretty much
the same kind of relationship to the communities in which
they lived as Simms did, and also that most of the better
southern writers of the twentieth century have had a relationship with their communities more or less like Faulkner's. It seems obvious that the modern southern writer
does not fall heir to the same kind of involvement within
a social community as his predecessors enjoyed, and it is
also pretty obvious, I think, that the quality of his literature at least has profited from the difference. For what the
twentieth-century southern author has offered is work that
at its best, though grounded in the life patterns of his community, has viewed that community *sub specie aeternitatis,*

as it were. Instead of taking care to display the home folks to the world as attractively as possible, he has sought to present them with the utmost moral and critical intensity of which he is capable. Instead of uncritically accepting the political, social, and ethical values of his community, he has conducted a continuing and often agonizing critique of those values. His art has been crafted out of a deep sense of familiarity with the texture of community life, but also of a momentous distancing of himself from that community. This has enabled him to peer into the depths and undercurrents of human life within the community not ordinarily visible or recognizable from the surface alone. The relationship with the home folks has been one of love and hate inextricably compounded, and like Quentin Compson at the end of *Absalom, Absalom!* he has found it difficult to categorize his complex feelings about the matter in mere abstract words, " 'I dont hate it,' Quentin said, quickly, at once, immediately; 'I don't hate it,' he said. *I dont hate it* he thought, panting in the cold air, the iron New England dark; *I dont, I dont! I dont hate it! I dont hate it!*"[43] William Gilmore Simms might well have understood how Quentin felt, but he would never have said it in print.

TWO

Mark Twain and the Postwar Scene

WE HAVE NOW TO DEAL WITH THE POST–CIVIL WAR LITERARY scene in the South. The figures who occupy it are almost all new. Between 1861, when the war began, and the 1870s, when the last troops left the South, there was an almost complete changing of the guard in southern literature. Only one or two writers bridge the two periods, and they are not the important ones.

Presenting the southern literary situation during those years between Appomattox Court House and the Spanish-American War is a difficult task, for the reason that the single most important fact about the period in the South was the shock and wound of that war—and yet the most important southern author of the period, Mark Twain, was not resident in that part of the region most affected by the war, and did not experience its impact in the same way at all. The only strategy that I can think of adopting, therefore, is to begin by discussing the shock of the war and its imprint on the southern literary scene, and then after that to turn to Mark Twain and deal with him. For in a sense the relationship of Mark Twain to the South is in important respects closer to that of the twentieth-century southern writers and the region than it is to that of his own contemporaries.

If we are to credit Thomas Nelson Page, the principal

34

reason why the literature of the antebellum South is now considered so lacking in distinction is that in that long-ago time, people talked literature instead of writing it. Page quoted Carlyle: "Literature is the thought of thinking souls." If this definition is accepted, he said, "the South was rich in literature. There was sufficient poetry and wisdom delivered on the porticos and in the halls of the southern people to have enriched the age, had it but been transmitted in permanent form; but wanting both the means and the inclination to put it in an abiding form, they were wasted in discourse or were spent in mere debate."[1]

Now of course Page knew better than that, and his essay, "Authorship in the South Before the War," does not stop with that claim but goes on to enumerate a series of explanations for the Old South's comparative literary barrenness, and most of them are sound enough. He did not slight the presence of slavery, and in another essay, "The Old South," he was even more explicit. That the Peculiar Institution had placed a shroud over the southern imagination, he was convinced. The South, he said, "held by its own tenets when they were no longer tenable, by its ancient customs when, perhaps, they were no longer defensible. All interference from the outside was repelled as officious and inimical, and all intervention was instantly met with hostility and indignation. It believed itself the home of liberality when it was, in fact, necessarily intolerant:—of enlightenment, of progress, when it had been so far distanced that it knew not that the world had passed by." And, he declared, "it was for lack of a literature that she was left behind in the great race for outside support, and that in the supreme moment of her existence she found herself arraigned at the bar of the world without an advocate and without a defense."[2] But (and having admitted as much, Page's address was mainly devoted to saying "but——")

Page did not accept for the South either blame for its adherence to slavery or guilt for its having attempted to secede from the Union. He was glad that slavery was gone, he said, but the Old South had even so been a beautiful and heroic establishment, and the task of the post-Reconstruction southern author was to see to the preservation of the Old South's reputation. The patriotic young southerner of today, he told his audience of college students in the late 1880s, "has before him a work not less noble, a career not less glorious" than those of his antebellum forebears. It was "the true recording of that story, of that civilization whose history has never yet been written—the history of the Old South."[3]

If that was indeed the true task of the postwar southern author, the success with which he discharged it was more marked along political and social than along strictly literary lines. Today the two southern authors who flourished between 1865 and 1900 and whose works are often read today for other than reasons of historical interest are Samuel L. Clemens and George W. Cable, and these are precisely the two who were least interested in proceding along the lines that Page laid out for them. We read Mark Twain today because he is one of the great literary artists of any time, and we read Cable because, though a considerably lesser artist, he wrote with more directness and prescience about racial discrimination in the nineteenth-century South than did any other southern author, even including Mark Twain. All the other literary lights of the period— Joel Chandler Harris, Mary Noailles Murfree, Sidney Lanier, James Lane Allen, Page himself—have long since dropped back into a relative obscurity. Posterity has not been kind to the local colorists. When the magazine vogue for local color went out in the middle 1890s, it left southern authorship stranded.

Politically, however, it was another matter entirely. The

enormous success of southern fiction in the post-Reconstruction years in accomplishing what Page considered its primary mission has been well documented. Statements to this effect range from Albion Tourgée's lament, in the 1880s, American literature had become "not only southern in type, but distinctly Confederate in sympathy,"[4] to the measured conclusion of the historian Paul H. Buck, in the 1930s, that

> for better or for worse Page, Harris, Allen, and their associates of the South, with the aid of Northern editors, critics, magazines, publishing houses, and theaters, had driven completely from the northern mind the unfriendly picture of the South implanted there in the days of strife. In place of the discarded image they had fixed a far more friendly conception of a land basically American and loyal to the best traditions of the nation, where men and women had lived noble lives and had made noble sacrifices to great ideals, where Negroes loved "de white folks," where magnolias and roses blossomed over hospitable homes that sheltered lovely maids and brave cadets, where the romance of the past still lived, a land where, in short, the nostalgic Northerner could escape the wear and tear of expanding industry and growing cities and dwell in a Dixie of the storybooks which had become the Arcady of American tradition.[5]

The story is well known how, in the years following the end of the Reconstruction, the freedman was abandoned by his northern liberators and left, landless and without education, to fend for himself, and how the nation looked the other way while the white South proceeded to enact into law a system of racial discrimination that ultimately reached into almost every facet of the southern community's political, economic, and social life. It was the rallying cry of "white supremacy" that ensured the Solid South, and that was used to destroy any political insurgency by

Populists or whatever that might threaten the status quo.
The role of the South's local color literature in preparing
the mind of the North for acceptance of the disfranchisement of the black man has also been well documented. To
use the Uncle Remus tales as an example, it is obvious that
the white folks who cared for the old man so fondly and
considerately, and who were in turn so trusted by him,
"knew" the black man better than meddling outsiders and
could safely be entrusted with his wellbeing. This may
not be what Harris consciously intended; it may not even
be what the stories themselves say if read by a discerning
modern critic; but it is what they were taken to mean. To
put the matter simply: in the eyes of the nation the image
of Uncle Remus replaced that of Uncle Tom. The black
character was the same in both instances; the difference
lies almost entirely in his relationship to the resident
whites, and vice versa.

There is a tremendous irony implicit here. Presumably
the South's defeat in the war and the emancipation of the
slaves liberated the southern writer from the requirement
of having to defend the South at every juncture, and allowed him, for the first time in many decades, to criticize
the foundations of southern society without having to
worry about the needs of sectional self-defense. Yet paradoxically the southern writer thereupon succeeded, as he
had not been able to do before the war, in importantly in-
fluencing northern opinion on the subject of the South's
racial arrangements, thus doing his part and more in helping to arrange matters so that the white South could dis-
franchise the black man. Freed, in other words, from the
need to write propaganda, he proceeded to produce it as
never before.

The reasons why this proved possible are not hard to
discover. For one example, by showing conflicts within
southern society, as his predecessors were forbidden to do,

a Thomas Nelson Page could create dramatic tension and then resolve the conflict in favor of the forces of virtue, thus demonstrating that in the Old South the virtue was predominant. Obviously this made for more interesting fiction. Similarly a Joel Chandler Harris could depict a happy and contented old black man enjoying the affection of his white folks, and since the relationship between them was apparently voluntary and not enforced, no one could say that the good feelings were irrelevant because the old black man had no choice in the matter. (That in point of fact he did have almost no choice did not dawn upon most members of the white American audience for many decades to come.) More important perhaps than internal story dynamics, however, were the general mood of the nation, the political situation in the post-Reconstruction era, the need of an urbanizing nation for an authentic pastoral image, and other such matters—including the fact that a defeated South now posed no economic and political threat to the industrial establishment north of the Potomac and could therefore be depicted favorably in fiction again. Whatever the reasons, southern local color literature, in particular that drawing upon and glorifying the plantation tradition, won a nationwide popularity that the antebellum writing had never enjoyed.

The popularity proved transient. When local color writing lost its popular vogue in the 1890s, the southern literary movement collapsed along with it. Such literary triumphs as were registered by southern authors during the years just before and after the turn of the century were mostly in the field of historical costume romance, in the manner of Mary Johnston. This literature was all but totally deficient in serious literary portraiture; it was bestseller stuff, devoid of genuine literary achievement. Not until the post–World War I years would there be such doing again in southern literary circles.

Why was it, one may wonder, that the resident southern writers played so negligible a part in the two leading schools (some say they are one) in American literature during the late nineteenth and early twentieth centuries—critical realism and naturalism? Why did not southern authors (with the notable exception of Clemens) follow the lead of Howells in producing a new kind of literature that, in the words of Robert E. Spiller, "gained philosophical depth from the theories of the new evolutionary science, understanding of the human consciousness from the advances in the infant science of psychology, social significance from the makers of systems of society who followed the Industrial Revolution wherever it went, and encouragement from a more intimate knowledge of contemporary French, German, Russian, and other continental European literature?"[6]

The answer, I think, is almost the same as for the antebellum period. Though the Old South was gone now, its habits of mind and heart, its sense of community identification were not. For, if theoretically the need to defend the Peculiar Institution no longer existed and the writers were free to examine their society, in practice there was now an even more binding force making for political and social orthodoxy. That force was the Lost Cause.

I have sometimes wondered why it is that no good historian has ever written a book specifically on the cataclysmic impact of the defeat of the Civil War on the South. The subject has been approached here and there, but no one has ever attempted to make a thoroughgoing investigation—economic, political, social, cultural, aesthetic—of what it meant to the South, in all aspects of its society, to lose the Civil War. No doubt the very magnitude of the task is a deterrent, for there is little in southern life that the subject would not somehow touch upon. Almost everything of importance that happened to the South in the half-century that followed the surrender of its armies is the result, in one way or another, of the downfall of the Old South on the battlefield. If the war gave the death blow to the old planter-dominated, precapitalistic society, at the same time it decisively retarded any chance that the South would develop industrially for at least three or four decades. The war wiped out slavery, and without the slave to work the land, the value of that land was vastly diminished. The only possible way whereby an agricultural community of landless slaves and moneyless landowners could continue to produce was through the inefficient and dreary sharecropping system. With no southern bloc of agrarian votes to prevent it, the northeastern manufacturing interest in Congress enacted a strongly protectionist tariff, and no longer was a staple crop exporting region such as the South able to buy freely on a worldwide free trade market. Cotton prices plummeted, and the rural South sunk into a financial ruin that left it saddled with the sharecropping system for decades to come. Except for a few "New South" manufacturing centers such as Atlanta, Birmingham, Richmond, and Charlotte, and except for a modicum of commercial enterprise in New Orleans and Jacksonville, the southern towns and cities, dependent as they were on the countryside, did not prosper or grow. The image that Henry Timrod, in "The Cotton Boll," had predicted would characterize New York once the Confederacy had triumphed:

There, where some rotting ships and crumbling quays
Shall some day mark the port which ruled the Western seas[7]

became a description of not only his native Charleston but of Norfolk, Savannah, Mobile, and New Orleans as well. The South's colleges and universities were mostly all closed for years following the end of the war, and when they re-

opened there were few who could afford to attend them.
Tax revenues for public education were inadequate at
best, and were rendered doubly so by the cost of maintaining dual school systems for black and white.

It was in those years that the South's old system of aristocratic leadership and noblesse oblige, most of its power
now gone, broke down, and the Upcountry white farmers
of what before the war had been the nonslaveholding sections began to assert themselves politically. For now that
the rural South was forced to compete in the American
capitalistic marketplace, the theories and attitudes of a
planter-dominated aristocratic government were not ade-
quate to shelter and protect the small farmer from the
rigors of a protectionist, finance-dominated economic system, and the result was a wave of agrarian unrest that cul-
minated in Populism and the emergence of the Upcountry
into political power.

Paradoxically this extension of popular democracy
meant, for the black southerner, the end of any participation in government, for with the coming of the common
man into power came the imposition of rigid racial segregation and the disfranchisement of the black voter. Any
chance—and at best it was slight—that the black man
might have slowly but steadily been allowed by the white
South to raise himself to full citizenship and participation
had been nullified by the shock of the Reconstruction, and
equally any chance that the North might have succeeded
in forcing a biracial democracy on the white South had
proved illusory, for northern public opinion simply was
not behind such an effort. The economic difficulties that
arose in the West and the North during the 1880s made
the northern financial community much more concerned
with securing southern conservative help against the threat
to its continued control over the government than with
seeing to it that the freedman was given his civil rights.

As for the white South, confronted as it was with the presence of many millions of uneducated, illiterate former slaves, it faced a social problem of vast proportions. Given the bemired condition of the mass of blacks and the profound depth of racial prejudice in both North and South, the best that probably could have been hoped for during these years was an arrangement something like that in the northern cities, whereby the blacks would be given token political participation, with the door held open just wide enough to permit the possibility of advancement for such members of a black middle class as might be able to manage it. But here the old community structure of southern society, still in existence after the war as before, helped to prevent the working out of any such arrangement. For the very fact that the southern community was not rigidly divided into separate economic classes, and afforded its members the personal participation and role identification we have noted in the Old South, worked now to help bring about total segregation. Accustomed to a society that dealt less in economic relationships than in individual role identity, the southern white could not conceive of the kind of token participation by a rudimentary black middle class, as existed in the economically-compartmentalized northern cities. If the former slave were allowed to take part at all, such participation would, the whites believed, be so thoroughgoing and so pervading that it would involve what to a white man of the nineteenth century was unthinkable: full and complete social integration of the races in the southern community.

To prevent this, the white South proceeded to force upon the black South a system of racial discrimination, in law as well as in fact, that penetrated every aspect of individual and community identity, cruelly inhibited the development of a black middle class, and held the mass of the black population into a condition of virtual economic and social peonage. Unable to conceive of civil liberties for the black man except in the ultimate terms of all or nothing at all, the white South banded together to see that he got nothing.

Obviously so great a problem as the South's racial relations would have been difficult to handle well even under what were otherwise the best of conditions. But as it was, conditions were anything but ideal. Economically, politically, socially the South was in dire shape. To say, as Walter Hines Page did, that the region lay in a state of spiritual shock is not far from the truth.[8] Bled by the war, stripped of its wealth, stunned by the defeat of its ambitions and the rebuke to its hopes, it was a stricken, tragic land. A perceptive outsider, Henry James, noted this upon visiting Richmond and the seaboard South as late as 1904: "I can doubtless not sufficiently tell why, but there was something in my whole sense of the South that projected at moments a vivid and painful image—that of a figure somehow blighted or stricken, discomfortably, impossibly seated in an invalid-chair, and yet fixing one with strange eyes that were half a defiance and half a deprecation of one's noticing, and much more of one's referring to, any abnormal sign."[9] Had the novelist gone to Atlanta, perhaps, stayed at the still new Kimball House, read the recent paeans to the new (and still mostly imaginary) industrial South composed by the heirs of Henry W. Grady, he might have reached a different conclusion, but somehow I think not. James was a discerning man, and would have seen the claims of a prosperous New South of commerce and industry for what at the time they still were—something along the line of Mark Twain's Colonel Sellers and his family seated around a coal stove on a chilly night with only a tallow candle burning inside the stove to give, through the isinglass window, the illusion of a warming fire. Industrial development did not make important trends in the South until the 1900s, and the region remained a place of thread-bare, economically stagnant, politically and socially conservative, closely joined communities.

This is the period of southern history, I think, about which we really know least. There has been ample investigation of the Populist revolt and of the coming of rigid racial segregation, to be sure, but no one has tried successfully to delineate the close-knit texture of the southern community as it was in the 1880s and 1890s. We have primarily the testimony of a few novelists such as Cable, Harris and Page, and all were trying, in one way or another, to prove something. Cable's *John March, Southerner,* the only truly realistic portrayal of the post-Reconstruction South, came closest perhaps to showing how it was, but Cable was writing about a north Georgia community, not about the New Orleans he knew so well, and he tended to focus upon specific political and economic issues rather than upon the texture of community life. The outlines that have been drawn by scholars of a later day, I think, have customarily been too harsh, too simplified. In their emphasis on class conflict, racial problems, and agrarian discontent they have left out the essential quietude and torpor, the unexamined pieties and loyalties, the role-playing, the tranquility that must have survived into the new day for all the dreariness of poverty and the violence of racial and class conflict. The community identity that characterized the Old South did not disappear with Lee's surrender; otherwise there could not have been so much of it remaining up into our own day, as the testimony of the southern writers of the twentieth century indicates that it was. It was still strong enough, in the late decade of the nineteenth century and the beginning of the twentieth, to hold its young people. No *Spoon River Anthology* seems to have come out of it, no *Main-Travelled Roads.* It would be members of the generation born at or near the turn of the century who would undertake such explorations, and even then they would tend to paint the outlines of the southern community of their childhood in the lurid colors of tragedy and the extravagant hues of comedy, not in the bleak drabness of the midwestern realists and naturalists.

The late decades of the century, then, were a period of ties still binding and allegiances still fierce, in which a defeated society sought on the one hand to hold onto its old forms and on the other to adjust itself to the demands, however inglorious, of a gradually-changing way of life. Until the end of the century at least, the emblem of those loyalties, ties, and resentments was the Lost Cause. Every town had its Confederate memorial statue, its set days for memorial commemoration and speechmaking, its corps of ageing veterans and its old women with long memories. The look was backward: to a time of heroic military defense and heartbreaking defeat, and beyond that to a time before the war when the community of the Old South had flourished and given social definition to the lives and characters of its members. Mark Twain noted the obsession (for it was all of that) when he visited New Orleans in 1882. "In the South," he wrote in *Life on the Mississippi,* "the war is what A.D. is elsewhere; they date from it. All day long you hear things 'placed' as having happened since the waw; or do'in' the waw; or befo' the waw; or right aftah the waw; or 'bout two yeahs or five yeahs or ten yeahs befo' the waw or aftah the waw. It shows how intimately every individual was visited, in his own person, by that tremendous episode. It gives the inexperienced stranger a better idea of what a vast and comprehensive calamity military invasion is than he can ever get from reading books at the fireside."[10] As Walter Hines Page wrote in his pseudonymous novel, *The Southerner,* the war gave every survivor of it "the intensest experience of his life and ever afterward he referred every other experience to this. Thus it stopped the thought of most of them as an earthquake stops a clock. The fierce blows of battle paralyzed the mind."[11]

The Confederate heritage, then, served as a kind of identity in itself, a fusing of individual loyalties with that of the community, a symbol of a harrowing experience commonly experienced. The South looked back to glory, and whatever the southern community encountered in the present that it did not like, it could attribute to the results of the war. There was an orthodoxy of Confederate valor and southern sacrifice that, because it was solace and explanation for a present-day economic, political, and social reality that was often all too ignoble, proved very durable indeed, possessing and marking the imagination of two generations of southerners. All the young men and women who grew up during those times and began to write books were affected by it; they were linked to the collective consciousness of their community by ties that were not only as binding as those that hold the writers of the Old South, but in addition were knotted in the psychological pain of shock and defeat. The martial past held the imagination in rigid bondage; the southern writer of the late nineteenth century could not and would not look around him, but only backward. The getting out from the constriction of those bonds would be the story of the twentieth-century southern literary renascence.

"What is it?" [Shreve McCannon asks Quentin Compson in *Absalom, Absalom!*] "something you live and breathe in like air? a kind of vacuum filled with wraith-like and indomitable anger and pride and glory at and in happenings that occurred and ceased fifty years ago? a kind of entailed birthright father and son and father and son of never forgiving general Sherman, so that forever-more as long as your children's children produce children you wont be anything but a descendant of a long line of colonels killed in Pickett's charge at Manassas?"

"Gettysburg," Quentin said. "You cant understand it. You would have to be born there."[12]

Only two men, Samuel L. Clemens and George W. Cable, of all the southern writers who began publishing stories and poems in the years that followed Appomattox Court House, were able to escape the trauma of the Lost Cause. And really only Clemens did, since Cable did not so much escape it as spend a lifetime struggling against it, and for all his effort his art remained prisoner to it. For though Cable, alone of his generation, conducted a defiant struggle against southern racial injustice, and though he was eloquent in his castigation of southern atavism and indolence, his imagination remained largely bound to the topical terms on which such issues presented themselves as a result of the war, and he did not probe beneath those issues into the depths of heart and mind. In even his best fiction there is a resort to sentimentality where we might expect introspection (whether conscious or unconscious introspection it does not matter very much), and the result is that he stayed on the surfaces and could not give his fiction the controlling form that comes of meaning perceived from within as well as without.

Thus it is Mark Twain, and Mark Twain alone, whose imagination was sufficiently free to look within himself. By accident of birth and heritage, Samuel Langhorne Clemens was able to compose, out of the division and confusion of his engagement in his time and place, a few works of literature that offer the moral ordering and spiritual affirmation of great art. From Hartford, Connecticut, and Elmira, New York, Mark Twain could look at the South and at himself with the vision of discovery.

Since he is the South's premier literary artist of the nineteenth century, it is upon him and his work, and their oblique but essential relationship to the South, that I want now to concentrate such critical artillery as I am able to train upon the subject.

Duplicitous Mark Twain, Leslie Fiedler calls him, observing within his books divisions and contradictions that go deep within the American psyche.[13] Concerning the South, Samuel L. Clemens was indeed a deceiver.* He was born there, he grew up there, he even enlisted in its military defence in 1861, and he wrote his greatest books about the life he knew there. And there were times when he admitted as much. But at other times he wrote in anger of southerners as "them," carefully avoiding on such occasions the use of the first person plural; and often he went to considerable trouble to assert his sympathy with things northern and his distaste for things southern. His disguise was aided by the circumstance that he first came into the national limelight in the middle 1860s not directly out of the South but by way of the Far West, and the image of the man as a "California bull" in the eastern china shop, sending the genteel pieties crashing all about him, is one that has persisted.

"That part of him that was western in his southwestern origin Clemens kept to the end," his friend William Dean

* In deference to the warning issued by my colleague and spiritual adviser, Mr. Lewis Leary, I attempt throughout to use the penname "Mark Twain" to refer to the authorial personality and the name Samuel L. Clemens to refer to the biographical author, for as Mr. Leary points out, "Mark Twain was a character who inserted himself, sometimes with joyous abandon, into almost everything which Samuel Clemens wrote."[14] In fairness to Mr. Leary, who though married to a southern girl has nought but Yankee blood within his arteries, I should make it clear that he does not share my opinions on the southern identity of Mark Twain. "I am not as convinced as several of my friends are," he writes, "that Mark Twain is genuinely southern, though perhaps Samuel Clemens was, from whose brow Mark Twain sprang full-blown in California when Clemens was almost thirty."[15] But if Mark Twain is the literary invention of Samuel Clemens, and if Samuel Clemens was a southerner, just where does that leave us? Perhaps it leaves us with the conclusion that Mark Twain is not a southerner, but a southern invention. I will settle for that, trademark and all.

Howells wrote, "but he was the most desouthernized southerner I ever knew."[16] But Howells was referring to his
notorious denunciations of slavery and of the southern
pesudo-Gothic ideal—and certainly there was more to being a southerner than that, as is suggested in Howells' description of the last day of his last visit with his friend at
Stormfield:

> The last morning a soft sugar-snow had fallen and was
> falling, and I drove through it down to the station in the
> carriage which had been given him by his wife's father
> when they were first married, and had been kept in hon-
> orable retirement all those intervening years for this final
> use. Its springs had not grown yielding with time; it had
> rather the stiffness and severity of age; but for him it must
> have swung low like the sweet chariot of the Negro "spir-
> itual" which I have heard him sing with such fervor, when
> those wonderful hymns of the slaves began to make their
> way northward. *Go Down, Daniel* was one in which I can
> hear his quavering tenor now. He was a lover of the things
> he liked, and full of a passion for them which satisfied it-
> self in reading them matchlessly aloud. No one could read
> *Uncle Remus* like him; his voice echoed the voices of the
> Negro nurses who told his childhood the wonderful tales.
> I remember especially his rapture with Mr. Cable's *Old
> Creole Days,* and the thrilling force with which he gave
> the forbidding of the leper's brother when the city's survey
> ran the course of an avenue through the cottage where the
> leper lived in hiding: "Strit must not pass!"[17]*

---

* Howells aside, I admit to a certain discomfort in considering Samuel
Clemens as a southern writer. The discomfort arises not because a discussion on such terms is inappropriate—quite the contrary; but because
of the presence, to this day, of a heritage of patriotic critical zeal that
has bedevilled so much southern literary scholarship in the past. That is
to say, discussing Samuel Clemens as a southern writer should limit the
universality of his art no more than discussing James Joyce as an Irish
writer should limit Joyce's, but in actual practice when one must deal
with a figure such as Clemens or Poe one always suspects oneself of falling
into the old chauvinistic trap of seeking to extol the virtues of the South

Discussions of whether Clemens's literary imagination was importantly southern or not tend to get involved in what are often irrelevancies. Was Hannibal, Missouri, a southern or a western town when Sam Clemens was living there? Was Missouri a southern or a western state back then? Was a pilot's life on the Mississippi before 1861 southern in its forms, or was it western? How serious was Clemens's ideological involvement with the Marion Rangers? Does Mark Twain use the English language in the way that William Faulkner does, or more as Sherwood Anderson and Ernest Hemingway do? Is the theme of the revolt from the village a southern or a midwestern theme? And so on. These matters have their bearing on the problem, but are not central to it. What is central is the forms that the imagination took, and how the imagination was formed.

We tend, when we begin speaking about the South as a social entity, to think in terms of a part of the South, and then to treat that part as the whole. Politically there has been some justification for doing this, though it seems to be vanishing, but in most other respects it is a risky business. C. Hugh Holman identifies three distinct modes of southern consciousness, related to three distinct subregions, and he cautions us that "however shadowy the lines of demarcation among them may be and however similar many of their attitudes were, they dreamed different

---

by claiming for it the work of writers who would enhance its reputation as a producer of writers. Goodness knows the temptation to do so is strong, for the nineteenth century at least, since otherwise one might be obliged to satisfy one's regional pride with Henry Timrod and William Gilmore Simms. But it works the other way around, too. One can demonstrate one's emancipation from the moonlight and magnolia school of criticism by refusing to acknowledge any claims of southern identity for a Clemens or a Poe, and in the middle twentieth century, surfeited as it still is with the reverberations of Confederate rhetoric, that too can be an occupational hazard for a critic of southern literature. For myself I elect to essay the first-named risk. I do so because I know of no other way to explain Mark Twain and his art, both for better and for worse.

dreams, formulated different social structures, and worshipped different gods. These differences have persisted for a century and a half and they give evidence of being qualities permanent to their various locales."[18] Mr. Holman defines these subregions as the Tidewater, the Deep South, and the Piedmont South. In the last-named, he says, the "society is in many ways more nearly American and less distinctively southern, except for its grotesquerie," than in the Tidewater and the Deep South, and he points out that unlike the writers of the latter two locales, the writers of the Piedmont have judged their homeland by a standard which, "whether it be that of social justice, or religious order, or of moral indignation, has always been an outer and different standard from that embraced by the local inhabitants." He notes Thomas Wolfe's use of the standards of the middle western writers. "Freed from the deep emotional commitment typical of the Tidewater and the Deep South," he declares, "Wolfe could look calmly and critically at his region, deplore its weaknesses, and love its strengths, without indulging in the emotional upheaval over this ambivalent attitude which Quentin Compson suffers in *Absalom, Absalom!*"[19]

Though Mr. Holman would not include Samuel L. Clemens within the geographical boundaries of his southern tryptych, he has suggested, as I see the matter, an interesting access to Mark Twain. The farmlands of eastern Missouri are not part of the Piedmont, but in the days when Sam Clemens was growing up there, they were surely the border South. Hannibal, Missouri, was settled by southerners, it was linked economically to the river and was dependent upon the trade up and down the river, it was a slaveholding community, and when the war broke out it was largely secessionist in sentiment. Its interests, tastes, and attitudes, if we are to believe Dixon Wecter and others who have studied its life, were notably southern—even to the extent that its bookshops offered for sale the *Southern Literary Messenger,* which the *Hannibal Journal* described in 1848 as being far superior to "the wishy washy concerns that issue from the eastern cities."[20] Hannibal was certainly not part of the Tidewater or the Deep South; it was a part of the westward migration from those places. But as De-Lancey Ferguson reminds us, "Mark Twain was also a son of the South. To think of him in terms of the Nevada mining camps where he made his first literary reputation, to think of his youthful homes as they look to a New Yorker of today—as too many of his critics have done—is to miss the strongest forces of his life. Hannibal, Missouri, cannot be interpreted in terms of that rebellion against village and farm which began with Ed Howe in the 1880s and Hamlin Garland in the 1890s. The society Mark Twain lived in was not ours; it must be thought of in terms of its own dreams, not ours."[21]

Samuel Clemens's father, John Marshall Clemens, was a Virginian and a Whig, who before coming to Missouri lived in Kentucky and Tennessee, holding in Tennessee title to considerable land which to his dying day he expected would one day make his family rich. Jane Lampson Clemens, Sam Clemens's mother, was of Kentucky stock. Like her husband she believed in the rightness of slavery throughout her life. "She had never heard it assailed in any pulpit," her son tells us, "but had heard it defended and sanctified in a thousand; her ears were familiar with Bible texts that approved it, but if there were any that disapproved it they had not been quoted by her pastors; as far as her experience went, the wise and the good and the holy were unanimous in the conviction that slavery was right, righteous, sacred, the peculiar pet of the Deity, and a condition which the slave himself ought to be daily and nightly thankful for."[22]

In a notable passage in *The Flush Times of Alabama and*

Mississippi, Joseph Glover Baldwin describes the difficulties that the Virginians had in the frontier South of the 1830s and 1840s, set down as they were, men of honor and pride, among the less scrupulous and less prideful plain folk. "Superior to many of the settlers in manners and general intelligence," Baldwin writes, "it was the weakness of the Virginian to imagine he was superior too in the essential art of being able to hold his hand and make his way in a new country, and especially *such* a country, and at *such* a time."[23] In many respects Baldwin might have been writing about John Marshall Clemens. Dignified, reserved, a man of probity with a high sense of civil role, conscious of his status and of his ancestry, he was respected by his fellow Missouri villagers, but he met financial ruin when he involved himself with a man of considerably humbler origins and stature who however was able to inveigle Clemens into a disastrous business transaction. Clemens had owned a few slaves: ultimately he was forced to sell them all. He wasted $200 of the family's money on a fruitless trip to Tennessee and Mississippi to collect a debt; he could not bear to foreclose on a man who owed him money (and who was apparently fairly well off) , but he had no qualms about taking a black man along and disposing of him for ten barrels of tar.[24] When his wife reproached him upon his return for his failure, he tried to justify himself and then, with a "hopeless expression" on his face, added, "I am not able to dig in the streets."[25] But his eldest son, Orion, was forced to go to work as apprentice in a print shop, and at first the comedown involved in having to perform manual labor chagrined the son. As for Sam Clemens, he was too young to go to work then, but when his father died in 1847 he too found a job as helper in a print shop.

I have no intention of reciting Samuel L. Clemens's biography, but I wanted to make the point that right here at the outset, in the boyhood of Sam Clemens's life, we have the situation that would become the hallmark of his humor: the awareness of status and the effort to maintain it. Here is the southern family of good standing, minor aristocracy fallen upon evil days, seeking to hold to status and noblesse oblige in a more crass and democratic society where aristocratic pose comes close to being quixotic gesture, and high-minded scruples of honor the vulnerability whereby the vernacular land speculator with no such scruples could bring the man of honor down to poverty and ruin. And here is the youth Sam Clemens, admiring and wanting to believe in the heroic gesture, the aristocratic pose, and yet observing its practical ineffectiveness and its weakness, and experiencing the deprivation and embarrassment that it brought to those dependent upon it. In Mark Twain's work the public pose, the claim of the gentleman's privilege to special treatment and respect, is always being contrasted with the levelling processes of a disrespectful vernacular society. If we read from the letters that Sam Clemens wrote back to Hannibal in those years of the mid-1850s when he went off to St. Louis and the northeast as journeyman compositor, we will get the sense of the young man straining to assert the well-born pose amid the plebian circumstance away from home. In his writings so much that happens in the fiction and the fact (and the "fact" is often fictionalized) revolves around the question of status, and more particularly the public recognition of status. Colonel Sellers always maintains his role, at whatever cost to credibility. Tom Sawyer constantly strives to "be somebody" in the eyes of the community, and stakes everything on the "theatrical gorgeousness" of his performance. "We can't let you into the gang if you ain't respectable, you know," he warns Huck. In *Life on the Mississippi* the town boys envy the deckhand his privileged status, and the cub pilot covets the rank and dignity of the estate of piloting. In *Huckleberry Finn* a poor white boy finds it difficult to humble himself before a black man; two rogues pretend to be visiting nobility; a colonel stares down a lynch mob and berates their commonness. In *A Connecticut Yankee* a master mechanic from Connecticut becomes The Boss and takes down the king and knights of England a step or two. In *The Prince and the Pauper* an urchin changes places with a king. In *Pudd'nhead Wilson* the York Leicester Driscolls, Percy Northumberland Driscolls, and Cecil Burleigh Essexes cling to their privileged roles as best possible, while a slave woman brags to her mulatto son that he comes from the best blood of Virginia.

Mark Twain constantly makes humor out of this consciousness of status. "Who *is* I? Who *is* I?" declares a black man at a New Orleans dance in *Life on the Mississippi*, "I let you know mighty quick who I is! I want you niggers to understan' dat I fires de middle do' on de *Aleck Scott!*"[26] But it was no joke that led the noted humorist Samuel Clemens to reply, when Howells cautioned him not to write "up" to the prestigious *Atlantic Monthly* readership, that "it isn't the Atlantic audience that distresses me; for *it* is the only audience that I sit down to in perfect serenity (for the simple reason that it don't require a 'humorist' to paint himself striped & stand on his head every fifteen minutes)."[27] *He* was no coarse funnyman, he was assuring Howells, but a writer of taste and refinement. And there was the night when, having made an audience roar with delight all evening, he groaned to his reading tour companion George W. Cable, "Oh, Cable, I am demeaning myself, I am allowing myself to be a mere buffoon. It's ghastly. I can't endure it any longer."[28]

To the end of his life he openly sought the public recognition that he was something grand and special. Happily he recounted how the policeman in Vienna recognized him and ordered him past the barricade, saying "For God's sake let him pass. Don't you see it's Herr Mark Twain?"[29] When he received his honorary degree from Oxford, he wore his scarlet doctoral robe proudly, and thereafter displayed it on every possible occasion, remarking that he wished he could wear it around all the time. All through his life he required the external signs of privileged position to keep him convinced that his rank and dignity were real. "His favorite recreation in New York," Justin Kaplan tells us, "when he was not playing billiards was to stroll up and down Fifth Avenue in his white suit, chat with the police, and be stared at."[30] It was as if he never quite believed it, was never completely assured of his status. The doubt, and the need to prove his claim to importance, stayed with him to the finish. He confessed as much, albeit obliquely, in his speech at the farewell dinner tendered him in 1907 by the Lord Mayor of Liverpool, when he quoted Richard Henry Dana's anecdote of the skipper of the little coaster sloop who had a habit of hailing all passing ships "just to hear himself talk and air his small grandeur," and who hailed an inbound Indiaman, only to hear its majestic identification of itself, "the *Begum,* of Bengal, one hundred and forty-two days out from Canton, homeward bound. What ship is that?" The skipper of the sloop could only squeak back humbly, "Only the *Mary Ann,* fourteen hours out from Boston, bound for Kittery Point—with nothing to speak of!" For an hour of each twenty-four, Mark Twain told his English well-wishers, he lay alone at night with the realization that he was only the *Mary Ann,* fourteen hours out, with vegetables and tinware, but

> during all the twenty-three hours my vain self-compla-
> cency rides high on the white crest of your approval, and
> then I am a stately Indiaman, ploughing the great seas
> under a cloud of canvas and laden with the kindest words
> that have ever been vouchsafed to any wandering alien in
> this world, I think; then my twenty-six fortunate days on
> this old mother soil seem to be multiplied by six, and I *am*

the Begum of Bengal, one hundred and forty-two days out
from Canton, homeward bound.[31]

It is a beautiful conclusion, and the imagery is revealing,
for Samuel Clemens sometimes saw himself very well.

It needs no Freudian psychologist to suggest how importantly the figure of John Marshall Clemens possessed
his son's imagination—the proud Virginia-born father unable "to dig in the streets," whose life ended with his family moved in over a friend's drugstore and the family furni-
ture sold to pay debts. We see him repeatedly in Samuel
Clemens's fiction: as the pathetic and amiable Colonel
Sellers, as the masterful but blood-feuding Colonel Grangerford and the mob-defying Colonel Sherburn, as the several versions of aristocracy in *Pudd'nhead Wilson,* and elsewhere. Yet, interestingly enough, Clemens seems always
to have avoided placing such a figure in a direct father-son
relationship with his protagonists. Tom Sawyer, of course,
has no living father; his only competition for the limelight
is with his brother Sid. Huck Finn's father is a vicious old
poor-white reprobate, who however is satisfactorily killed
in mid-novel though Huck is spared the knowledge until
the close. Even in *Pudd'nhead Wilson* he could not let
Judge Driscoll be the actual father to Tom Driscoll; the
judge adopts his dead brother's son, and the matter is addi-
tionally complicated by the secret of Tom's actual illegiti-
macy. Of Sam Clemens's relationship with his own father
we are told that it was distant: "a sort of armed neutrality,
so to speak," he described it.[32] But Mark Twain's lifelong
love-hate fascination with men of aristocratic bearing, especially when southerners, surely grows out of that relationship. Of Judge Driscoll in *Pudd'nhead Wilson* he
writes that "in Missouri a recognized superiority attached
to any person who hailed from Old Virginia; and this person was exalted to supremacy when a person of such na-

tivity could also prove descent from the First Families of that great commonwealth." The Virginian, he says, "must keep his honor spotless. . . . Honor stood first."[33] But honor was no protection against the willingness of one Ira Stout to use the bankruptcy law and ruin the Clemens family,* and honor did not prevent Orion and then Sam from having to go to work in a print shop, and honor caused a slave girl who had been in the Clemens family for years to be sold down the river. Honor, particularly when viewed in retrospect, clearly had its limitations.

In *Huckleberry Finn* we encounter Colonel Granger-ford: "His hands was long and thin, and every day of his life he put on a clean shirt and a full suit from head to foot made out of linen so white it hurt your eyes to look at it. . . . There warn't no frivolishness about him, not a bit, and he warn't ever loud. He was as kind as he could be—you could feel that, you know, and so you had confidence. Sometimes he smiled, and it was good to see; but when he straightened himself up like a liberty-pole, and the lightning begun to flicker out from under his eyebrows, you wanted to climb a tree first, and find out what the matter was afterwards."[35] But this same Colonel Grangerford could take part in a stupid and bloody feud against the Shepherdsons, killing young men and boys, without concerning himself with the human consequences. John Marshall Clemens could serve as judge and justice of the peace, a pillar of rectitude, but he could sell a slave downriver, and trade another for ten barrels of tar. It was, in short, splendid to be a Virginian and an aristocrat—if you had no conscience to plague you for your sins.

As for the son, *he* had a conscience, all right; he felt guilt constantly, tormenting himself with it even when no guilt

---

* Wecter reports that town records show no record of such an incident, but he notes that various pieces of evidence do indicate the likelihood that something of the sort occurred.[34]

actually existed. Guilt for having given matches to an old drunk in jail, who promptly set fire to the jail and was burned to death; guilt for burlesquing old Captain Isaiah Sellers' newspaper column in New Orleans and shaming the old man into stopping his harmless pontificating; guilt for having allowed his younger brother Henry to be given too large a dose of morphine after the *Pennsylvania* explosion, so that he died; guilt for having violated the purity of Livy Langdon's sheltered Elmira existence with his rough, uncouth, ungenteel masculine love; guilt for having taken his young son Langdon out driving, so that he contracted diphtheria (sic) and died; guilt for having squandered Livy's inheritance and his own vast earnings so that he had to plead bankruptcy; guilt for having fathered Susy Clemens so that she could die a horrible death of meningitis, and Jean Clemens so that she could die of epilepsy; guilt for having once believed in slavery; guilt for the insult to Emerson, Longfellow, and Holmes in the Whittier birthday-dinner address; guilt for the loss of his literary powers; guilt for being a member of the "damned human race"—small wonder that Sam Clemens raged against his Presbyterian conscience, slew it in print so often, and in "The Mysterious Stranger" brought Little Satan to Hannibal (moved to Germany for the occasion) in order that the son of the Arch-Fiend might teach Tom and Huck that the absurdity known as the "moral sense" was at the root of all men's suffering. "No one, I think," Bernard DeVoto has written of Clemens's paper entitled "What Is Man?," "can read this wearisomely repeated argument without feeling the terrible force of an inner cry: Do not blame me, for it was not my fault."[36]

Literary psychologists have expended considerable effort attempting to trace down the sources of Samuel L. Clemens's lifelong affinity for feeling guilty. The official biographer, Albert Bigelow Paine, described a scene at the time of John Marshall Clemens's death. His son Sam, says Paine, was fairly broken down. "Remorse which always dealt with him unsparingly, laid a heavy hand on him now. Wildness, disobedience, indifference to his father's wishes, all were remembered; a hundred things, in themselves trifling, became ghastly and heart-wringing in the knowledge that they could never be undone." Jane Clemens took her son up to the room where his father lay, told him that what had happened did not matter now, and asked him to promise her to be a faithful and industrious man, like his father. That night Jane Clemens and her daughter were awakened to find a form in white entering their room. "Presently a hand was laid on the coverlet, first at the foot, then at the head of the bed." It was Sam, sleepwalking. "He had risen and thrown a sheet around him in his dreams. He walked in his sleep several nights in succession after that."[37] What Paine does not say is that apparently young Sam Clemens, peeping through a keyhole, had watched a doctor perform a postmortem examination on his father. As Wecter notes, doubtless the shock of his death and the guilty secret of the postmortem had more to do with the "heavy hand" of remorse and the somnambulism than any deathbed promise to his mother to be a good boy.[38]

What I am attempting to establish is not the nature of the guilt* so much as the fact that evidently it had considerable to do with Samuel Clemens's ambivalent feelings toward John Marshall Clemens. The consciousness of his "wildness, disobedience, indifference to his father's wishes," the "hundred things, in themselves trifling" which could nevermore be undone, must indeed have made him feel his inability to hold proper respect for his father's stoic dignity and to emulate it. He feared his father, he

---

* For a survey of the long history of critical dispute over the nature of Mark Twain's "wound," see Lewis Leary, "Mark Twain's Wound: Standing with Reluctant Feet," in *Southern Excursions.*

resented his father, and if he felt awe and admiration, he also felt some contempt. Sam Clemens could not muster, for the memory of John Marshall Clemens and what he stood for, the kind of unquestioning respect that he shows Colonel Grangerford as receiving in *Huckleberry Finn.* He did not believe in it, or at any rate believe in it enough to live by it. His father was not only the lordly Colonel Grangerford; he was also the impractical Squire Hawkins and the unworldly Colonel Sellers of *The Gilded Age;* and the judge of *Huckleberry Finn* whose sentimentality delivered Huck over to his father's sordid brutality; and the credulous King Arthur of *A Connecticut Yankee* who allowed Merlin to hoodwink him so thoroughly; and every other gentleman of aristocratic pretensions who proved either culpable or vulnerable, or both, in a wicked world.

In Mark Twain's day there was a literary tradition, or more precisely a subliterary, journalistic tradition, which was based squarely on the humor implicit in the confrontation of gentlemanly refinement and breeding with the vernacular shrewdness and realism of the new country beyond the Appalachians. The tradition had moved westward with the southern frontier—from Longstreet's rural Georgia, to Baldwin's flush times in Alabama and Mississippi, to Thorpe's big bear of Arkansas. It was not the Literature of the Old South and the Northeast; it did not draw on the plantation stereotype and the chivalry of Sir Walter Scott; its language convention was not that of the historical romance. But it was equally a part of the southern experience, and always had been. It was to this literary mode that Samuel Clemens instinctively turned, composing squibs in the print shop of Orion Clemens's newspaper, and later scribbling tales while in various places West, East, and South, as well as in the pilot house of steamboats on the river. He was always writing something, his teacher and crony Horace Bixby remembered. And had Clemens been only a journalist, only a southwestern funnyman, that is doubtless the vein he would have worked the rest of his life. But he was not merely a comic journalist. He was Samuel L. Clemens, for whom being funny was not enough. He went West for a few years, then East, and each of his books, as Henry Nash Smith shows so convincingly, steadily deepened their exposure of the values that lay beneath the comedy upon the surface.[39] The little village of Hannibal became St. Petersburg, and then Dawson's Landing and Hadleyburg, and finally Eseldorf. The gap between the real and the ideal, at first merely humorous, grew into a chasm that laughter could no longer bridge, until the rage at its failure to do so turned into a desperate effort for transcendence, the attempt to convince oneself that "you perceive, *now*, that these things are all impossible, except in a dream. You perceive that they are pure and puerile insanities, the silly creations of an imagination that is not conscious of its freaks—in a word, that they are a dream, and you the maker of it."[40] At such times the best thing to do is try to console yourself with the thought that, for twenty-three hours a day anyway, in the eyes of the world you are no small thing, but the *Begum,* of Bengal, one hundred and forty-two days out from Canton, homeward bound.

What has this vision to do with the South? Why, simply everything, it seems to me. What we have is a situation in which the private experience of the author matches so perfectly the public meaning of the time and place that the concerns of the one serve to exemplify and embody the problems of the other. Henry Nash Smith has shown how the art of Mark Twain involves a developing exploration of the potentialities of the vernacular democratic culture as a replacement for the Official Culture of the eastern seaboard, with its European models, and of how this exploration was embodied in language. In an early work such as *Innocents Abroad,* the vernacular values of the narrator clash with traditional cultural attitudes toward the art, history, and sacred institutions of the Old World. In *Tom Sawyer* the genteel narrator serves only as a frame, with the chief narrative focus placed on the direct description of Tom's experience in the village. In *Huckleberry Finn,* through using for persona the viewpoint of a youth whose relationship to polite society is peripheral and disaffiliated, Mark Twain moves into a critique of the professed values of the society. The contradictions between the idealistic pieties and inflated rhetoric and the realities of selfishness, repression, sentimentality, and brutality are given ever more savage exposure, until the story threatens to turn into a tragedy, so that the author must yank it back into burlesque. Is not this process, with its developing tension between aristocratic and democratic, genteel and vernacular, romantic and realistic modes, exemplified on the personal level in the child Sam Clemens's mixed admiration and contempt for the Virginian John Marshall Clemens, and on the historical, political level in the movement of the border South away from the aristocratic ideal of the old Tidewater? And does not the progressive discovery of the possibilities of the plain style, the "language of truth" as Lionel Trilling will have it,[41] embody in language the dynamics of the breakthrough from the windblown metaphor and ornate literary diction of so much Old South writing?

Mark Twain did not have to invent his style out of nowhere. The model was at hand—but in the subliterature and journalism of Old Southwest humor. What he did was to intensify and elevate this style into the full imaginative ordering of literature. That was his triumph, his great contribution to the development of American fiction. The midwestern realists of the 1890s and thereafter would adapt it for their purposes, but would use it for purposes of deliberate understatement; they would turn its simplicity into a means of depicting innocence betrayed, which was never Mark Twain's approach and was not what Huck Finn was about at all. The twentieth-century southerners would use it to cut away the excesses of the old high style and give sinew and strength to their sensuous documentation of experience. It is impossible to read a work such as "The Bear," or the better stories of Flannery O'Connor, for example, without seeing the example of the prose style of Mark Twain. With each step away from the literary language of genteel society Mark Twain moves away from the official pieties and values of the community toward a searching scrutiny of those values. To cite only one example of many such, the joyful community affirmation of the church service in *Tom Sawyer,* in which the congregation choruses "Old Hundred" when the supposedly drowned youths return in glory, becomes, when seen through Huck's eyes and with Huck's language, the hypocrisy of Miss Watson at prayer and the orgiastic sentimentality of the King at the camp-meeting (a scene drawn directly from southwestern humor by way of Simon Suggs).

We might profitably compare the camp-meeting scene to William Faulkner's portrayal of the Reverend Hightower and his relationship with the congregation in *Light in August.* Hightower perceives, at the end of the novel, that "that which is destroying the Church is not the outward groping of those within it nor the inward groping of those without, but the professionals who control it and who have removed the bells from the steeples."[42] Where Faulkner criticizes the perversion and prostitution of the religious values by those entrusted with their affirmation, Mark Twain suggests that religion and piety are hypocrisy and selfishness; when Huck decides that "All right, then, I'll go to hell!" it is organized religion itself that is found wanting. But here Mr. Holman's distinction is useful. Faulkner is of the Deep South, whose writers, like those of the Tidewater, "have found the standards to judge their societies in the ideals of their citizens, however little these ideals found firm expression" within the society itself, while Mark Twain is of the upper South, where "the standard by which it is judged, whether it be that of social justice, of religious order, or of moral indignation, has always been an outer and different standard from that embraced by the local inhabitants."[43] The border South of which Sam Clemens was a part was engaged, in Clemens's own time, in just such a breaking away from the aristocratic ideal of the Tidewater and the Deep South as characterized the Piedmont South of a later day, toward a more generally American frame of reference; and the movement of Sam Clemens away from Hannibal and onto the river and then to West and back East embodies the process of dislodgement. Not simply the values of the society being left behind, but the tensions of the breakaway itself, are part of the southern experience.

Yet one might well ask this: if what is important is the breaking away, the dislodgement, then at what point in the transaction does the original identity cease importantly to matter? Granted that Samuel Clemens was born into a southern community, does he not cease, fairly early in the development of his art, to be part of it?

The answer, I believe, is that the essence of the art *is* the breaking away, and is constituted of the tension between the pull of the old community and that of the forces separating the individual from it. In the art the separation can never really be effected, since the comedy and pathos of Mark Twain's work consist of the effort to separate and the effort to resist the separation, expressed most characteristically in the humor of incongruity. Here we have to watch Sam Clemens very carefully, for he was a master of disguise and duplicity. Consider the famed castigation of the Old South, the diagnosis of its Sir Walter Scott disease that caused fake medieval castles to be built in Baton Rouge and "created rank and caste down there, and also reverence for rank and caste, and pride and pleasure in them."[44] Huck Finn himself diagnosed the Sir Walter disease in this fashion: "So then I judged that all that stuff was only just one of Tom Sawyer's lies. I reckoned he believed in the A-rabs and the elephants, but as for me I think different. It had all the marks of a Sunday-School."[45]

Yet Mark Twain cannot end that novel without summoning back Tom Sawyer and his A-rabs and elephants, and in defiance of the laws of fictional probability must bring him back onto the scene for the Phelps Farm "evasion." And as for rank and caste, he has Colonel Sherburn step out into the squalor and mud of the main street of Bricksville and shoot an old drunk who abuses him, and then stand off a lynch mob, for all the world the defiant aristocrat who has contemptuously refused to be soiled by the riffraff. Sherburn tells the mob, with what can only be considered the full approval of Mark Twain (who has even shifted his persona from Huck to Sherburn for the purposes of delivering the speech), that

"I was born and raised in the South, and I've lived in the North; so I know the average all around. The average man's a coward. In the North he lets anybody walk over him that wants to, and goes home and prays for a humble spirit to bear it. In the South one man, all by himself, has stopped a stage full of men in the daytime, and robbed the lot. Your newspapers call you a brave people so much that you think you *are* braver than any other people—whereas you're just as brave, and no braver. Why don't your juries hang murderers? Because they're afraid the man's friends will shoot them in the back, in the dark—and it's just what they *would* do."[46]

The trouble with southern writing, Samuel Clemens tells us in *Life on the Mississippi,* is that it hangs onto its old, inflated style—"filled with wordy, windy, flowery 'eloquence,' romanticism, sentimentality..."—while the North has now discarded it.[47] But let me quote a three-sentence description of sunrise on the Mississippi from the same book:

> You have the intense green of the massed and crowded foliage near by; you see it paling shade by shade in front of you; upon the next projecting cape, a mile off or more, the tint has lightened to the tender young green of spring; the cape beyond that one has almost lost color, and the furthest one, miles away under the horizon, sleeps on the water a mere dim vapor, and hardly separable from the sky above it and about it. And all this stretch of river is a mirror, and you have the shadowy reflections of the leafage and the curving shores and the receding capes pictured in it. Well, that is all beautiful; soft and rich and beautiful; and when the sun gets well up, and distributes a pink flush here and a powder of gold yonder and a purple haze where it will yield the best effect, you grant that you have seen something that is worth remembering.[48]

It is not a bad passage at all, but it is a far cry from Huck Finn's way of putting things, though if Tom Sawyer had written the next book instead of Huck he would have said it pretty much like that. The point is that when Mark Twain sounds off about the South's reliance upon rhetorical embellishments, he is also chastizing an aspect of himself, and not something he has long since put permanently behind him. Tom Sawyer's way of building up his adventures so that they will provide "theatrical gorgeousness" is the way of Sir Walter Scott, and though Mark Twain pokes fun at it, the next minute he will turn around and do the same sort of thing himself. Let us not forget that the book that follows *Huckleberry Finn* is *A Connecticut Yankee,* which however it satirizes feudalism involves an exploit that Tom Sawyer himself would have been proud to bring off.

It seems to me that in *A Connecticut Yankee* the whole ambivalent love-hate relationship of Sam Clemens with the South is dramatized and laid out plainly. That the Arthurian England which Hank Morgan, master mechanic from Connecticut, sets out to reform is in effect the South of Clemens's youth, is clear from the very outset, as in the Yankee's description of the first town he sees: "In the town were some substantial windowless houses of stone scattered among a wilderness of thatched cabins; the streets were mere crooked alleys, and unpaved; troops of dogs and nude children played in the sun and made life and noise; hogs roamed and rooted contentedly about, and one of them lay in a reeking wallow in the middle of the main thoroughfare and suckled her family."[49] Give or take a detail or two, and that could be Hannibal, St. Petersburg, Bricksville, or Dawson's landing. Hank Morgan is appalled by the squalor and the torpor, and proceeds to show the king and the knights of the Round Table what Yankee know-how and democratic egalitarianism can do toward eradicating the feudal backwardness of Old England. It is not long before he has the knights going about on their errantry wearing advertising boards and with soap commercials on the trimmings of their noble steeds. At the crisis of his battle to eradicate feudalism he challenges a horde of armed knights to a battle to the death and pots eleven of them with his Colt revolvers, causing the others to break and flee. "Knight-errantry was a doomed institution," he exults. "The march of civilization was begun. How did I feel? Ah you never could imagine it." Thereupon he sets out to modernize Old England, and he does pretty well:

"Now look around on England. A happy and prosperous country, and strangely altered. Schools everywhere, and

several colleges; a number of pretty good newspapers.
Even authorship was taking a start.... Slavery was dead
and gone; all men were equal before the law; taxation had
been equalized. The telegraph, the telephone, the phono-
graph, the type-writer, the sewing machine, and all the
thousand willing and handy servants of steam and elec-
tricity were working their way into favor."

Even the stock market has been instituted:

Sir Launcelot, in his richest armor, came striding along
the great hall, now, on his way to the stock-board; he was
president of the stock-board, and occupied the Siege Peril-
ous, which he had bought of Sir Galahad; for the stock-
board consisted of the Knights of the Round Table, and
they used the Round Table for business purposes, now.
Seats at it were worth—well, you would never believe the
figure, so it is no use to state it. Sir Launcelot was a bear,
and he had put up a corner in one of the new lines, and
was just getting ready to squeeze the shorts to-day; but
what of that?[50]

As we know, however, it doesn't finally work. The medieval church, with its vast authority of superstition, pro-
nounces an interdict on the whole business. The supposedly democratized and liberated freemen revert to their
former state of cowed, timid slavery. Everything is shut
down, and ultimately the massed chivalry of Arthurian
England marches against Hank Morgan's fortress. With
horrible savagery the Yankee and his few loyal followers
blow up, electrocute, and otherwise annihilate the entire
establishment, their own citadel included. At the end only
the Yankee is left, to sleep for eleven centuries under Merlin's spell, awakening briefly in the nineteenth century to
die at last, lonely and lost, dreaming of a simple love in a
simpler time, long ago.

Henry Nash Smith has convincingly interpreted the tale as Mark Twain's fable of progress, and he identifies the terrible demolition at the close as an expression of the author's despair at the moral implications of the vernacular culture of the capitalistic nineteenth century. Because he could not finally discover a meaning for the society that has replaced what he had known and had rejected, he blew the whole experiment to smithereens. "He had planned a fable illustrating how the advance of technology fosters the moral improvement of mankind. But when he put his belief to the test by attempting to realize it in fiction, the oracle of his imagination, his intuition, the unconsciously formulated conclusions based on his observation and reading, his childhood heritage of Calvinism, at any rate some force other than his conscious intention convinced him that his belief in progress and human perfectability was groundless."[51]

What I find interesting is the striking appropriateness of the story and its outcome to the South that Sam Clemens knew—a relevance that Smith, and also James M. Cox (in *Mark Twain: The Fate of Humor*) have recognized. In effect it is a fable of the New South, as I see it. Is not that picture of the "happy and prosperous country" that Hank Morgan, the Yankee, creates out of the feudalism of Old England very much akin to the vision of the New South as advanced by Henry W. Grady, Marse Henry Watterson, and so many others during Samuel Clemens's times, and which would convert the former Confederacy into a replica of the industrial Northeast where the adult Samuel Clemens lived? Factories, schools, newspapers, commerce, all the modern inventions; slavery dead and gone, and the former knight-errants become stockbrokers who "used the Round Table for business purposes, now"—this is exactly how he described and praised the up-to-date aspects of commercial New Orleans in *Life on the Mississippi*. Every one of the improvements is cited, and praised, even down to the newspapers and the authorship. If only the entire South, he suggests in that work, would throw off its "Walter Scott Middle-Age sham civilization," its "sillinesses and emptinesses, sham grandeurs, sham gauds, and sham chivalries of a brainless and worthless long-vanished society," then it, like New England, might amount to something in the world.[52]

At times in *A Connecticut Yankee* he is explicit about the South's similarity to feudal England. Describing the callousness with which a group of pilgrims watched slaves being driven along a road, Hank Morgan comments, "They were too much hardened by lifelong every-day familiarity with slavery to notice that there was anything else in the exhibition that invited comment. That was what slavery could do, in the way of ossifying what one may call the superior lobe of human feeling: for these pilgrims were kindhearted people, and they would not have allowed a man to treat a horse like that."[53] Again, when Hank Morgan becomes disgusted with the way that oppressed peasantry instinctively sides with its noble oppressors, it reminds him "of a time thirteen centuries away, when the 'poor whites' of our South who were always despised and frequently insulted, by the slave-lords all around them, and who owed their base condition simply to the presence of slavery in their midst, were yet pusillanimously ready to side with slave-lords in all political moves for the perpetuating of slavery, and did also finally shoulder their muskets and pour out their lives in an effort to prevent the destruction of that very institution which degraded them."[54]

Yet when the railroads and the factories and the telephones come, when the Round Table becomes a stock market and money-making replaces knight-errantry and chivalry, the outcome is not what is hoped at all. Not at all. So that the author's attitude toward Hank Morgan seems to change. Toward the end the Yankee becomes more callous, and when having slaughtered 25,000 knights he issues congratulatory battle communiques that burlesque those of Napoleon and the generals of the Civil War, the Yankee has moved from being an emissary of progress and freedom into a smug, conceited, cold-blooded warlord himself. He has wiped out feudalism and slavery and backwardness, but at the cost of dehumanizing himself and becoming a symbol of the nineteenth century's much more efficient brand of military destruction. The arrival of industrial capitalism in the green fields of Old England has proved pretty much of a disaster.

One of the drawings that Dan Beard did for the original edition of *A Connecticut Yankee* is quite revealing in this respect. It illustrates an episode in which King Arthur, though he wishes to see how the common people live, refused the Yankee's suggestion that he learn to refer to a peasant as friend or brother. "Brother!—to dirt like that?" he asks. Beard provides a three-part drawing. The first shows a fat, bloated king, before whom a peasant in chains bows his head. The second shows an equally fat, bloated southern planter, complete with wide-brimmed hat and whip, with a black slave before him wearing a halter. The third shows a smug, officious-looking nineteenth-century businessman, with a working-man standing before him. Beneath the picture of the king is a sword, beneath that of the planter is a law book, and beneath that of the industrialist a group of money bags. Under each drawing appears the identical outline, three times repeated: "Brother!—to dirt like this?"[55]

I am not suggesting that in *A Connecticut Yankee* Samuel L. Clemens sat down to compose an allegory of the New South. What I am saying is that he envisioned feudal England in terms of the Old South, and set out to show how it could be made into a garden with the coming of

progress, industrial development and democracy, only to
realize at the end that the nineteenth-century industrial
capitalism of northeastern society was no valid alternative—whereupon he destroyed the whole thing in his rage
and frustration, and ended with a lonely old man dreaming of a simpler past, and very much out of place in the
modern world. The confusion of the fable, I believe, comes
directly out of Samuel Clemens's southern origins, and its
roots go all the way back to the Hannibal days. We can
observe the results all too clearly in the episode in which
Hank Morgan tries to tutor King Arthur in the ways of
imitating the manner and bearing of the peasantry. For
such purposes, he says, "your soldierly stride, your lordly
port—these will not do. You stand too straight, your looks
are too high, too confident. . . . Wait, please; you betray
too much vigor, too much decision; you want more of a
shamble. . . . You see, the genuine spiritlessness is wanting;
that's what's the trouble."[56] The intent of the passage, and
of several others, is to show that the peasantry has been so
beaten down by oppression that its members are cowed and
defeated. But what goes wrong is Samuel Clemens's ambivalent attitude toward aristocracy; he admires King Arthur's dignity and manliness so much that it becomes a
matter not of upbringing but of inherent kingly character.
King Arthur is a *king;* it is inborn in him, and Samuel
Clemens admires just that kingliness, even though the implications happen to be disastrous for his social theorizing.
Arthur is a king *because* he is kingly, and he will not compromise. One is reminded of Clemens's description of his
father, as "Judge Carpenter," in his unpublished "Villagers of 1840–3": "Silent, austere, of perfect probity and
high principle: ungentle of manner toward his children,
but always a gentleman in his phrasing—and never pun-
ished them—a look was enough, and more than enough."[57]
This kind of figure appears constantly in Mark Twain's
fiction.

One could go on, but there would be no point to it. The southern experience of Samuel L. Clemens is so thoroughly and deeply imaged in his life and work that one may scarcely read a chapter of any of his books without encountering it. It was, after all, no callow youth, but a twenty-four-year-old man, who quit the Marion Rangers and joined his brother Orion for the journey out to the silver fields. How much more important to Sam Clemens the issues and loyalties of the Civil War must have been than he pretends they were in "The Private History of a Campaign that Failed," in which the Confederate enlistment is depicted simply as a lark by unthinking boys. Surely it went deeper than that. Cox ascribes Clemens's later zeal to identify himself as a loyal Radical Republican to the zeal of a popular humorist to have the approval of his audience, and his fear that such approval would be withheld if his southern past were known. Until the "Private History" was published in 1885, Cox declares, "the Civil War had been the great unwritten experience in the tall tale of his past. Moreover, it had been not simply forgotten, but evaded— and evaded from the very beginning. The discovery of 'Mark Twain' in the Nevada Territory in 1863, while it had been Samuel Clemens's discovery of his genius, had quite literally been a way of escaping the Civil War past which lay behind him in Missouri. In effect, the humorous identity and personality of 'Mark Twain' was a grand evasion of the Civil War. His form, the tall tale, was a means of converting all the evasions and failures of Samuel Clemens into the invasions and excursions of Mark Twain. Thus aspects of the innocent, the gullible, the foolish, and the incompetent 'young' Mark Twain are rehearsed by the experienced and 'old' Mark Twain. Omitted in this humorous strategy is the transition between youth and age, failure and success, innocence and knowledge."[58]

And this, I think, is largely true. For the greatest art of Mark Twain is an art of childhood—Tom Sawyer in St.

Petersburg, the cub pilot learning his trade (but never practicing it), Huck Finn and Jim on the raft. "So endeth this chronicle," *Tom Sawyer* concludes. "It being strictly the history of a *boy*, it must stop here; the story could not go on much further without becoming the history of a man."[59] But into that childhood the author thrust the concerns of his adult years. *Tom Sawyer* is a "hymn to boyhood," but it is a boyhood in which the nostalgic image of an innocent childhood in a drowsing little town is made the scene of a young boy's determined battle for recognition and fame within the community, culminating in heroism, success, the accolades of the leading citizens, and wealth—money let out at 6 percent. It *must* end, all right, for what else could Tom do to maintain the delusion that the A-rabs and the elephants were all about him and not just the Sunday school? The riverboat cub pilot of *Life on the Mississippi,* significantly younger and more naive than Sam Clemens was when he learned his trade, masters his craft and becomes a pilot, but there the story ends, to be resumed one page and twenty-one years later when the former pilot turned author comes back to inspect the river again. Besides, now that the tugboats and barges have taken over, and the pilot's association has been outmaneuvered by the boat owners, "the association and the noble science of piloting were things of the dead and pathetic past!"[60] Huck Finn, who did not believe in the A-rabs and the elephants, flees from the conformity and hypocrisy of the village and sets out on a long voyage downriver, his companion a runaway slave. As the journey progresses, the exploration of the corruption of the society along the banks widens, culminating in Colonel Sherburn's denunciation of the mob and then the claustrophobic, suffocating presentation of ignorant cruelty and emotion-starved sentimentality that is the Wilks family episode. After that Jim is sold into captivity, and Huck makes his liberating decision: to disregard the "conscience" that his society has given him to distinguish between right and wrong, and to free his friend. But when he arrives at Phelps Farm, it is not really a Deep South farm that he finds: it is that of Sam Clemens's uncle John Quarles in Florida, Missouri,[61] only viewed not as the child Sam Clemens knew it but as it would appear to a Huck Finn. Using Huck for his persona, Clemens can see the country of his youth without the blinders of nostalgia. But Huck cannot *act*. So along comes Tom Sawyer and the great "evasion," and the terrible anticlimax at the close in which we learn that Tom has known all along that Jim was free.

Why that wretched undercutting? Why could not Mark Twain have let Tom help Huck to free the slave? Because Samuel Clemens knew only too well that the boy that Tom Sawyer symbolized would never, could never have set a slave free. Such was the continuing hold of his southern childhood upon Samuel Clemens's imagination. Huck might assume Tom's name at the farm, but Huck, with what he knew, could never *be* Tom. Yet Mark Twain had to become Tom again, in order to end the novel.

Artistically all that follows *Huckleberry Finn* is a comedown. In *A Connecticut Yankee* the Old South, with its feudalism and pseudo-chivalric ideal, is transformed into the postwar industrial society of the urban Northeast, but that does not work either, and must be erased in explosion and rage. In *Pudd'nhead Wilson* the drowsing village becomes Dawson's Landing, with its confused and hopeless nightmare of miscegenation, hypocrisy, and violence; black is white, white black; the upright Virginia-born judge is dishonored and murdered. It has not helped to change things around so that the enslaved man is white and the aristocrat is a Negro; for the slavewoman whose story it is, what matters in life has been destroyed: "Her hurts were too deep for money to heal; the spirit in her eye was quenched, her martial bearing departed with it, and the voice of her laughter ceased in the land. In her church and its affairs she found her only solace." Clemens is clearly unable to make any sense of the story; significantly, even the customary persona of Mark Twain is missing from the scene, appearing only in the calendar entries which serve as headnotes for the chapters. We are left with Pudd'nhead Wilson's cynical maxim for summation: *"October 12, the Discovery.* It was wonderful to find America, but it would have been more wonderful to miss it."[62]

He was born in the South, of a Virginian father and a Kentucky-born mother. He grew up in a little slaveholding village along the river, a village very much like others in the country beyond the Tidewater and the mountains, where in his own words, "there were grades of society: people of good family, people of unclassified family, people of no family. Everybody knew everybody, and was affable to everybody, and nobody put on any visible airs; yet the class lines were quite clearly drawn, and the familiar social life of each class was restricted to that class. It was a little democracy that was full of Liberty, Equality, and Fourth of July; and sincerely so, too, yet you perceive that the aristocratic taint was there."[63] *His* family, by birth and pretension at least, was of the aristocracy, and his father a lawyer and leading citizen of the village. But in that town and in that time and place, it was not enough to be an aristocrat; for this was not Virginia, but the border South, where the land was too cheap and people too much on the move to remain within the old patterns. Unable and unwilling to lower himself, as he must have seen it, to the requirements for prospering in that new country, John Marshall Clemens failed, and left his son a legacy of decline and fall, the pride of honorable bearing and the knowledge of its pathos and its inadequacy.

Had Samuel Clemens been born in the Deep South and

had things worked out there in the same way, the literary result might well have been the equivalent of the Quentin Compson of *The Sound and the Fury,* holding desperately to concepts of southern honor in a world of Snopeses and change, and finding a resolution only in tragedy. But this was the border South, and he was Sam Clemens of Missouri, who perceived the absurdity equally with the pathos.

Or to speculate further—always a risky business, to be sure—had he lived further south, the war might have caught him up in its magnitude—and God knows his father would have wanted it that way for him, once Virginia had been invaded—and left him trapped in the confusion and the shock of the defeated Confederacy. Instead he went West with his brother, became a humorist, and then came East, where he flung himself gleefully into the money-making frenzy of the Gilded Age, scheming to make millions with typesetting machines and kaolin compounds in much the same way that Tom Sawyer dreamed of pirate gold. But all the while the forces of his creative imagination held ferociously on, in hatred and in pride, to that faraway country of his youth. Again and again he sought in art to find in the play of his memory the order and meaning that would tell him who he was. In comedy he strove to articulate and resolve the tensions, incongruities, and contradictions that his restless self-scrutiny kept turning up. His great weapon was laughter. When finally it failed, he was left high and dry, dictating rambling memories to a secretary, along with furious but ineffective tirades against a hostile universe.

When we come to assess the place of Samuel L. Clemens in the story of southern literature, this much seems obvious. Clemens, as no one else in southern literature before the twentieth century, brought to bear upon the southern experience a critical scrutiny that enabled him to search below the surface pieties and loyalties and get at the underlying conflicts and tensions within the society. It seems safe to say that he saw these things so well because they were to be found within his own heart as well as in the life around him. No other southern writer came close to the liberation he achieved. He was able to do it for at least two reasons. The first was that by accident of time and place, he was jarred loose from the southern community in a way that none of the others were, with the social tensions involved therein present within his family and his society. The second reason, of course, was that he was Mark Twain.

He stands, with all his genius and his shortcomings, in a relationship to the society he knew that anticipates that of the generation of writers who came to literary maturity after the first world war. Not for decades after his time would there be other southern writers who would find themselves both tied to and dissociated from the southern community in something like the way he had been. When that day came, the twentieth-century southern literary renascence would be under way.

Let me close with an anecdote. In February of 1901 a gathering was held at Carnegie Hall in New York City to celebrate the ninety-second birthday of Abraham Lincoln. The purpose was to raise funds for the Lincoln Memorial University at Cumberland Gap, Tennessee. Colonel Henry Watterson, editor of the *Louisville Courier-Journal* and a leading propagandist for the New South of commerce and industry, was the featured speaker, and to introduce the noted Marse Henry the sponsors called upon a cousin of his, Samuel L. Clemens. Mark Twain opened with some humorous remarks, and then went on about how he and Henry Watterson, both of them ex-rebels, were, like thousands of other southern boys who had fought bravely for the flag they loved, proud to pay their homage to Abraham Lincoln, remembering only that "we are now indistinguishably fused together and namable by one common great name—Americans."[64]

It was a fairly standard reconciliation speech, one of many such made by many southerners during those years. The curious thing, however, is the pose that Samuel L. Clemens was assuming for that occasion. "We of the South are not ashamed," he declared, of having fought against the Union, for "we did our bravest best, against despairing odds, for the cause that was precious to us and which our conscience approved; and we are proud—and you are proud—the kindred blood in your veins answers when I say it—you are proud of the record we made in those mighty collisions in the fields."[65]

Knowing what we do of the several weeks of active avoidance of all possible collisions in the fields of Missouri that marked the entire Civil War record of Lieutenant Samuel L. Clemens of the Marion Rangers, what are we to make of that performance? Was he being ironic? What would Huck Finn have thought of it? God only knows. I doubt very much that Mark Twain knew himself.

THREE

The Writer in the
Twentieth-Century South

IN THE LAST OF THREE LECTURES ON THE WRITER IN THE
South, I want to turn to the writers of the twentieth-century southern literary renascence, and to inquire, in effect,
what there was in the condition of their relationship to the
southern community that enabled them to portray, as their
predecessors were largely unable to portray, the underlying problems of human meaning and definition lying beneath the surface of southern life, so that the best of them
could produce works of literature that could universalize
southern experience.

Rather than taking up the story with the year 1900 and
the developments in southern literature and life in the first
two decades of the twentieth century, however, my notion
is to begin by examining some of the implications of an
often-discussed and often-criticized book, entitled *I'll Take
My Stand: The South and the Agrarian Tradition*, which
appeared in 1930, just as the southern renascence had gotten into high gear. The participants in this volume were
poets, novelists, professors, men of letters; and the view of
the South and of their relationship to it that they assumed
represents, I think, an essential stage in the history of
southern literature.

I should like to begin with a story. Some years ago I was
visiting in Georgia with a friend of mine, a distinguished

scholar of American literature, and we were invited by the late John Donald Wade to have dinner with him in Marshallville. I had had some correspondence with John Wade through the offices of a good friend to us both, the late Donald Davidson, and of course I knew both his distinguished biography of Augustus Baldwin Longstreet and his essay, "The Life and Death of Cousin Lucius," which I still think the most beautifully written of the twelve essays in the Agrarian symposium, *I'll Take My Stand.* As for my friend, though he was an avowed Yankee from upstate New York, he was more than ordinarily interested in the South, and was in fact at work on what proved to be an excellent anthology of southern writing. So we got in my car and drove down through the peach orchards to Marshallville. We arrived in the middle of the afternoon, and of course it was no trouble to find out where Mr. Wade lived.

When we got there, Mr. Wade had company—two of his colleagues from the University of Georgia, one of them a noted southern historian whose many scholarly books were and still are standard works for anyone engaged in the study of nineteenth-century southern history, and the other an economist also distinguished in his field far beyond the boundaries of his campus. They were sitting around in Mr. Wade's living room, sipping Jack Daniel's from silver cups, and swapping stories. We joined them for awhile, and then John Wade took the two of us off in his automobile for a tour of his place. What we were shown was an arboretum, and, executed on a scale dozens of acres wide, a Garden of the World, with trees and shrubs trained on wire scaffolding to form Stonehenge, a Druid temple, the Eiffel Tower, a huge cross, and so on. My northern friend was astounded; he could not imagine working on a scale like this, and to such long-range purpose. It was an eighteenth-century sort of enterprise, he kept whispering to me. Afterward we returned to the house and rejoined the two Georgia friends of John Donald Wade, who had been improving the hour in our absence, and we spent the next four hours helping them in their endeavors toward yet further improvement, with time out for dinner. Mr. Wade and his companions were good raconteurs. They kept telling stories to each other, one after the other, and laughing uproariously at every opportunity, slapping their sides and the like at each quip and sally. Their stories were about people around home. They told them in good southern fashion, with lots of drawling and contracting of syllables—"Well, by Gawd, ah jes said to ole Bill . . ." and "Man, lemme tell you bout what old Charlie Jones said when . . ." and "well if that don't beat anything I ever heard tell . . ." and so on—and if you hadn't known that the story-tellers consisted of a distinguished literary scholar and editor, a distinguished historian, and a distinguished economist, you might have thought that they were members of the local farming community thereabouts. In any event it was a most amusing evening, concluding about nine p.m. or so with a ceremonial tribute to the camellias just off the porch, and then my northern friend and I said goodbye and we climbed back into my automobile and were soon on the way to Atlanta.

No sooner had we gotten out of the driveway and driven down the street than my northern friend began expressing his astonishment. "Did you *hear* that?" he asked. "Why, did you *hear* them? Going on like that, talking like *countrymen?* Why, what do you make of it? And there he was with that *garden,* that obviously would not possibly be *completed* for another fifty years. . . . Why, you would never have *guessed* who they *were!* It was absolutely *incredible!*" and so on.

Obviously he had never encountered anything remotely like it before. But I had recognized what was going on right away. What dear old John Wade and his two distinguished academic colleagues were doing was demonstrating to each other, but most of all to themselves, that they were still southern boys. They were, to put a more formal construction upon it, asserting their community identity. For there they were: three southerners who had grown up in much the same way as other southerners of their time, but who had then gone off to college and to graduate school and had become scholars in universities. They had taken part not only in the intellectual enterprises of their own campuses but in those of the American and even world-wide scholarly community as a whole, and they had written learnedly and wisely on matters abstruse and profound. They were scholars and intellectuals of a very high order, having achieved widespread success in their chosen academic disciplines, honored members of the scholarly community—and yet they all felt just a little uneasy in their allegiance to such a community, and for all their achievement and renown, they wore their academic robes a trifle uncomfortably. Ideas and theories and researches did not seem quite real to them, for they still had a vivid memory of another kind of reality, a different kind of community identity, in which individual people and not ideas were what were considered most real, and in which the participants were not set off into academic disciplines and scholarly fields, or professions and occupations and economic brackets, but were part of a society made up of various kinds of men and women with all kinds of jobs and interests and different levels of education, a society to which they too had once belonged. They had left that kind of community when they had gone off to college and become scholars, and they had done so by their own choice, but all the same they still remembered that earlier community and the kind of real-life identity it had afforded its members, and no matter how absorbing their intellectual careers and how important a part of the scholarly world they were, they missed that kind of identity, still, and felt a bit strange and unworldly without it. So now that they could get together over a drink with old friends whom they trusted, each was doing his best to reassert it, to show each other and, again, himself most of all, that he was still part of it and it was still part of him.

As I say, my northern friend was baffled at this. He felt no such inclinations himself; he did not have to prove, either to himself or to others, that he was one of the boys. He was quite satisfied with being a scholar and a university professor: that was all the real life he craved. He could not understand why it was that three such noted scholars would want to seem anything other than noted scholars, or why they might find stories about what ole Bill Smith said and what ole Charlie Jones did "real," in a way that ideas and intellectual concerns were not. But as for me, as I say, I was not puzzled at all. I knew what they were up to all too well. I had seen myself doing much the same sort of thing from time to time. For I too was from the South, and wore my own intellectual identity just a trifle uneasily.

I do not want to make too much out of this incident (I may already have done so) except that the more I think of it the more it seems to me that what it offers is an insight, however amusing in this instance, into one of the central dimensions of the literature of the modern South. It is emblematic, I think, of a relationship of the southern man of letters to his society, and out of this relationship has come important qualities for the literature he has composed.

I think not only of "The Life and Death of Cousin Lucius," in *I'll Take My Stand*, but of another of John Donald Wade's essays, that on southern humor, which he contributed to a volume entitled *Culture In the South*, published in 1934.[1] In this essay John Wade was discussing

the lineage and the prevalence of humor in southern literature, and he portrays an imaginary Christmas dinner in the
year 1932, to show how the spirit of the old frontier humor
of Judge Longstreet and others survived as a form of social
life. He describes a gathering of several generations of a
family and friends, and he details their occupations. There
are a farmer, a small town merchant, a lawyer, doctors,
merchants, a mail carrier, a teacher, a knitter of bedspreads,
a cousin who is curator of an art gallery in Chicago, a
Sorbonne-trained teacher of French at Vassar, and so on.
He proceeds to show them telling stories "that mail-carry-
ing Uncle Jack and Proust-teaching Cousin Julius will
both think pointed."[2] And he gives the participants in this
imaginary Christmas dinner, some of them names that
doubtless belong to members of his family, but some of
them the names of persons whom I recognize as fellow
Nashville Agrarian and other Vanderbilt associates of John
Wade. I notice that there is John, a Caroline, a Red, an
Andrew, and doubtless others that someone more knowl-
edgeable than I could readily identify.

The moral that John Wade drew from this imaginary
Christmas feast is that southern humor historically was and
is yet based on the sense of individuality of the participants, and much of the joy arises not from the story being
told as such (which all the others have often heard before)
but of the effect based on the existence of a social tradition
"which insists that human beings must quite inescapably
remain humorous if they are to remain human, and one
may well believe that it will reassert itself."[3]

What I find most interesting about the passage is its self-
consciousness. It seems to me that what John Wade was
attempting to do was to demonstrate that though, to choose
one example of several such, Red Warren was just back
from being an Oxford student, his truest kinship did not
lie in his intellectual Oxford identity but in that which he

shared with the farmer and the mail carrier. Now of course
there is considerable truth to this, but not all the truth.
The world in which Cousin Julius, the Proust scholar of
the anecdote, lives is not nearly as populous with Proust
scholars as it is with mail carriers and farmers, and the social and political units in which we participate and by
which we govern our relationship with the society we live
in are not so specialized that Proust scholars consort only
with other Proust scholars, or even only with other scholars
of whatever sort. Universities exist within larger societies,
are functioning parts of larger societies, and what happens
in universities will depend, for better or for worse, on the
attitude of the larger societies to them. But the tendency
in the twentieth century has been for those specialized
units within our society—the university, the mail carriers
union, the retail merchants association, the bar association—to become increasingly important in themselves and,
through sheer density of population numbers if for no
other reason, to become more and more self-absorbed. The
Proust scholar has less and less to say to the mail carrier,
and vice versa. Their dependence upon each other, and
their relationship to each other, becomes purely economic,
and for the most part rather impersonally so.

In the account that John Wade proposes, however, the
relationship is not merely economic, but personal and fa-
milial. So at the imaginary Christmas dinner the Proust
scholar tells a story that the mail carrier will find amusing,
and presumably the mail carrier tells a story that the Proust
scholar will find amusing, since they are both, by virtue of
family and society, in a social relationship. But—to continue this tenuous probing behind the assumptions of a
good essay—if we think about the Christmas gathering that
John Wade sketches for us, what draws the two of them
together for this social relationship is only a ceremonious
occasion, Christmas dinner. The Proust scholar teaches at

Vassar, the art gallery curator lives in Chicago, the female novelist lives in New Jersey; we may guess that the mail carrier works the RFD route there in Marshallville, the merchant runs the dry goods store there, the doctor practices in Atlanta, the lawyer in Macon, and so on. Their gathering, then, is a reunion, and what links them and makes them interested in each other is not what they are now, but what they were in the past, when the mail carrier and the Proust scholar and the lawyer and the art gallery director were all growing up with the others in the community of Marshallville.

I said that what struck me most about the passage was its self-consciousness. What I mean is that John Wade is *asserting*, in his essay, that Uncle Julius the Proust scholar and Miss Mary the Chicago art gallery curator and Cousin Red the just-returned Oxford graduate are at bottom not intellectuals but just plain folk like the mail carrier and the merchant, and he is making an *intellectual argument* to support the contention. What he was doing was maintaining that in the South, Proust scholars and authorities on the sculpture of Jacob Epstein were not wandering intellectuals but members of an organic community involving people in all walks and levels of life. He was suggesting, too, that in such a community the man who studied Proust belonged equally and was equally at home with and valued with the lawyer, the doctor, the merchant, the farmer, the mail carrier.

But the truth, I am afraid, is the other way around. I suggest that the mail carrier at that dinner would hesitate not one whit in talking about delivering mail, nor the doctor about treating patients, nor the merchant about the price of eggs, because they would assume (and rightly) that all the others would know what was involved and have opinions in it, while the Proust scholar would never think to talk about the Baron de Charlus, because he would know that the mail carrier, the lawyer, the doctor, the merchant, and the farmer would have not the remotest idea of who the Baron de Charlus was or why he was of any importance whatever. The best he could do, no doubt, would be to talk about the university football team's fortunes during the past fall. To the extent, then, that Cousin Julius was a Proust scholar, he was *not* part of the society. But— assuming that Cousin Julius or someone like him was writing the essay—what he was attempting to do was to *use* his intellectual powers to set forth an interpretation of society from which he would not be separated.

I have gone into this matter because of the light it sheds, as I see it, on the Agrarian symposium, *I'll Take My Stand*. In his essay "Remarks on the Southern Religion," in *I'll Take My Stand*, Allen Tate asks the question, "How may the southerner take hold of his Tradition?," by which he means the heritage of his nonindustrial, historical, concrete, community-shared attitude toward nature and man. His answer is, "by violence."[4] The remark has been widely misunderstood. What I, at any rate, take him to mean is that the southerner, in Mr. Tate's view, must consciously and even abstractly *will himself* back into his tradition of community identity, even though the essence of such a tradition is that it is automatic and unconscious. It seems to me that there, as so often, Mr. Tate gets right at the true point of issue, and that he is simply stating what *I'll Take My Stand* is all about, and also setting forth quite clearly the anomaly involved in the whole venture. For when the twelve southerners set forth their Agrarian manifesto in 1930, what they were in effect attempting to do was to formulate a theory of a southern society that would still have room within it for themselves. If the South was indeed to become the Agrarian community that they favored, there would no longer exist the dissociation of sensibility that had brought about their very separateness as writers and intellectuals, for then what was now a theory of the good community would *become* the community. The very existence of *I'll Take My Stand* was emblematic of the breaking up of that once organic community; had southern society continued to provide the human identity within the southern community that had once existed, there would not have resulted the self-consciousness that led the contributors to write their essays.

Thus John Wade's imaginary Christmas dinner scene, composed as it was by someone who was aware of the extent of the separation of himself from the southern community gathered for the dinner, was an effort to will away that separation through an intellectual formulation of what that community was. It was an *assertion of identity,* an assertion made necessary precisely because the identity was, in part at least, no longer present. The separation of the southern writer from the southern community had by the 1920s proceeded to the extent that the writers who were moved to compose the essays of *I'll Take My Stand* felt impelled to formulate a view of the nature of that community in which the occasion for such separation would not exist. They took for their model the society of the Old South (and, in its less threadbare aspects, that of the late nineteenth-century South), and what they said in effect was: this is what the southern community should have been, and what it must come back to being if we are to avoid any more of the fragmentation and the dissociation that characterize modern urban life and that are already rapidly destroying the southern community. They were able to recognize that incipient disruption because they saw it within themselves: because they were already sufficiently distanced from the community to be made conscious of what that community had been and was not, in reference to themselves as writers.

It is in this light, and not as a political or economic document, that I interpret *I'll Take My Stand.* Its opposition to industrial society is based on the belief, on the part of the contributors, that man in an industrial society is involved in a progressive enslavement to economic production, which is bound to result in his dehumanization, and which makes impossible through its economic specialization and social compartmentalization any individual identity and sense of "role" within a community of individuals. By contrast, to quote from the opening Statement of Principles,

> Opposed to the industrial society is the agrarian, which does not stand in particular need of definition. An agrarian society is hardly one that has no use at all for industries, for professional vocations, for scholars and artists, and for the life of cities. Technically, perhaps, an agrarian society is one in which agriculture is the leading vocation, whether for wealth, for pleasure, or for prestige—a form of labor that is pursued with intelligence and leisure, and that becomes the model to which the other forms approach as well they may. But an agrarian regime will be secured readily enough where the superfluous industries are not allowed to rise against it.[5]

What the twelve southerners were saying, in effect, is that under industrialization as it exists in twentieth-century America, society is exploitative and predatory, because it is organized with a view toward ever-increasing economic production and material consumption, and so cannot provide harmony and individuality within a stable community. In a nonindustrial society, by contrast, the organization and the direction of the society are necessarily settled and established, anchored as they are to the land, so that those who live in such a society may belong to a lasting community of individuals and can define themselves in and by its permanence.

A great deal of the impetus behind the writing of *I'll*

Take My Stand, it seems to me, came out of this sense of community breakup, with its resulting collapse of the individual role within the community. Those who read the volume as an attempt to call back into existence the historical Old South by a deliberate turning toward mass subsistence farming miss the point (though it must be said that several of the essays in the book encourage such a misreading). In its essentials the book was a protest against the kind of community that seemed all but inevitable if industrialism were allowed to transform the South into an urban-dominated industrial society. With the example of the urban northeast exposed before them, the Agrarians saw the South in the process of changing into a replica of the impersonal, economically-organized, soulless metropolis, in which the individual citizen was little more than a statistic of consumption and production.

From their standpoint the southern community which had existed during their childhood and young manhood, before the first world war, was still very much preferable to such a society, in that it afforded the citizen an individual identity, one in which relationships between individuals, because personal, were characterized by manners and amenities. And since the southern community was historically a product of the Old South, which had been avowedly anti-industrial and had resisted, politically, socially, and ultimately militarily, the encroachment of industrial capitalism, it was only natural that the Old South would serve the twentieth-century Agrarians as a symbol for the kind of community they advocated. In addition they were drawn, by virtue of history and community loyalty, toward a defense of the southern tradition, and they saw the historic hostility of the South toward the North in terms of the preservation of the nonindustrial, mannered, leisurely style of life, with its possibility for individual identification, against the menace of urban industrial capitalism. As

Robert Penn Warren expressed it at the Fugitives' reunion
in 1956, reminiscing about how the Agrarians had become
involved in their project: "the machines disintegrate individuals, so that you have no individual sense of responsibility and no awareness that the individual has a past and
a place. He's simply the voting machine; he's everything
you pull the lever on if there's any voting at all. And that
notion got fused with your own personal sentiments and
sentimentalities and your personal pieties and your images
of place and people that belong to your own earlier life.
And the Confederate element was a pious element, or a
great story—a heroic story—a parade of personalities who
are also images for those individual values. They were
images for it for me, I'm sure, rather than images for a
theory of society which had belonged to the South before
the war. . . . For me it was a protest . . . against certain
things: against a kind of dehumanizing and disintegrative
effect on your notion of what an individual person could
be in the sense of a loss of your role in society."[6]

It is precisely this quality, I feel sure, that has accounted
for the continuing popularity and importance of *I'll Take
My Stand* over the course of some forty years, in the face of
the manifest fact that neither the South nor the rest of the
country was interested in holding onto an agrarian economy, and while industrialism and urbanization were growing by leaps and bounds from the Potomac to the Gulf of
Mexico. The volume was a protest against dehumanization, a rebuke to the mass-produced society of urban industrialism, and a plea for the retention of human values and
individual identity within a community. In such a transaction the Old South and the agrarian existence served as
a metaphor for the good life. Nowadays, over the distance
of four decades, much of what the twelve southerners were
saying in regard to the predatory nature of unchecked industrialism and the dehumanizing tendency of unrelieved

large-scale urban existence has turned out to be extremely prophetic and all too relevant. Several decades before what was thought by many to be no more than the ineffectual lamentation of some impractical neo-Confederates over the passing of the golden age of slavery, turns out to be the first stages of a widespread revolt against computerized, depersonalized, machine-oriented society and its ruthless exploitation of the environment and its human inhabitants. After years of being considered backward-looking reactionaries, the twelve southerners now begin to look remarkably like prophets.

This is not to say, of course, that *I'll Take my Stand* is not in certain important respects an outdated book. Because a precapitalistic, agricultural society was the only kind of society that the twelve southerners were able to conceive of as offering an alternative to industrial capitalism, they tried their protest against dehumanization too closely to an outmoded economic system, when in fact the actual economic arrangements were really subordinate to the main thrust of their argument, which was not so much profarming as antimetropolitan. The specific agricultural emphasis, instead of being allowed to remain metaphorical, gave their polemic a backward, antiquarian look, when in reality they were well ahead of their time in facing up to the problems of an urban, industrial society that a future generation would ultimately be forced to confront.

Furthermore their reliance upon the southern experience for their image of an organic, harmonious community meant the acceptance of the South's racial arrangements, and thus seemed to involve the perpetuation of economic peonage and second-class citizenship for the black southerner. The South's version of the harmonious community had traditionally been for whites only, and *I'll Take My Stand* did not question this assumption (though it must be said that Warren's essay, "The Briar Patch," placed so much rhetorical emphasis on the importance of the "equal" in "separate but equal" that it greatly disturbed several of his fellow contributors). The effectiveness of *I'll Take My Stand* as a protest against dehumanization was therefore compromised by the injustice it seemed to acquiesce in for black southerners—again, as so often in the past, a southern effort at resistance to industrial dehumanization was crippled by the attempt to defend the indefensible. The truth was that in the choice between agricultural peonage in the sharecropping system in an overly racist society, and urban discrimination in the wage system of an impersonal, economically fragmented society, the black man had more to gain by the latter, since in it there was at least some chance for him to advance toward more advantageous terms of participation in society. The twelve authors were thus trapped in the historical dilemma of the South. "I thought," Warren recalled, "we were trying to find—in so far as we were being political—a rational basis for a democracy. That, I thought, is what we were up to."[7] But unless such a rational basis could be shaped to include black men as well as white, it would be to that extent irrational and undemocratic. The only way to resolve the dilemma would be to include the black man as an equal participant in the traditional community, and that, in the year 1930, was beyond the capabilities of most white southerners, including the participants of *I'll Take My Stand*.

Enough, however, of the feasibility, or lack of it, of the program as set forth in *I'll Take My Stand*. It was a polemical work, written in the late years of the 1920s and published in 1930, just as the nation was sinking into the Great Depression. The indictment it drew up of post–World War I American industrial capitalism was given considerable force at the time by that circumstance, for by the time the book appeared the economy of the country seemed to be heading rapidly into just such a disaster as the Agrarian critics had intimated was inevitable if it were allowed to continue its ways unchecked.

The Great Depression came just as the South appeared to be climbing out, to an extent at least, from the defeat and shock of the Civil War and the Reconstruction. I have already noted that it was not until about the turn of the twentieth century that the region showed signs of importantly throwing off the shock—economic, political, social, spiritual—of that defeat. As measured by the instruments of historians and social scientists, the South would appear to have begun, about 1900 or thereabouts, to recover some of its former agricultural, commercial and industrial power. Henry W. Grady's New South of commerce and industry, no more than a forlorn hope in the 1880s, now became something more substantial. The industrial revolution, delayed first by slavery and then for long decades by the impact of the defeat of the war, began arriving in force. Southern cities grew, and southern manufacturing increased to an extent that a substantial portion of the southern population was no longer tied to the land. Public education was vastly expanded, and a few southern colleges and universities became for the first time important centers of learning. Mass communication expanded into the hinterland, along with highways. After the election of Woodrow Wilson the South for the first time since the coming of the Civil War enjoyed a modicum of genuine political power and influence in the national government.

With the coming of the first world war the South once again knew real wealth, for money flowed in from the North and West in the wake of army training cantonments and widespread construction of industrial plants to produce the materials for war. Hundreds of thousands of northerners and westerners came South, both as troops to be trained and as workers to take advantage of the need for skilled labor in the new factories. Similarly hundreds of thousands of southerners went North and West, so that the insularity of the old southern community was shattered. In the words of an historian, "the ubiquitous war economy gave the region a taste of affluence such as it had never before experienced, and lifted economic expectations to levels from which they would never again completely recede. Industry expanded, farm prices rose, and workers, even sharecroppers, became acquainted with the feel of folding money."[8] The end of the war did not mean an end to growth and change. Though in the 1920s farm prices sagged and there were ominous signs of difficulties to come, the business expansion continued, the suburbs grew, and the South's reentry into the union was confirmed. Highways linked the hinterlands to the towns and the cities. Mass communication penetrated into the backcountry. Vast numbers of black southerners left for the northern ghettoes. The Confederate veterans were all dead or dying. The fabric of southern social life was significantly disrupted. The political domination of the rural South was undercut. Villages became towns, towns became cities. Old habits of belief and attitude, the pieties, prejudices, and values of a closed, fixed, unchanging society were importantly confronted by the needs, demands, and opportunities of a more cosmopolitan, eclectic, changing life.

In the year 1926, just four years before *I'll Take My Stand* appeared, the chairman of the English department at that very university that would soon provide the nucleus for that Agrarian symposium published a book proudly entitled *The Advancing South,* and he ended that volume with a prophecy:

No one can have too high a hope of what may be achieved within the next quarter of a century. Freed from the limitations that have so long hampered it, and buoyant with the energy of a new life coursing through its veins, the South will press forward to a great destiny. If, to the sentiment, the chivalry, and the hospitality that have characterized southern people shall be added the intellectual keenness, the spiritual sensitiveness, and the enlarged freedom of the modern world, the time is not far off when scholarship, literature, and art shall flourish, and when all things that make for the intellectual and spiritual emancipation of man shall find their home under southern skies.[9]

What Edwin Mims thought when he was handed a copy of *I'll Take My Stand* four years later has not to my knowledge been recorded. One hopes, albeit faintly, that he had the wisdom to recognize that, however much the Agrarian symposium attacked just the kind of uncritical attitude toward modernism that his own book exemplified, the very existence of *I'll Take My Stand* represented something of a fulfillment of his prophecy. For in it a group of southern writers were displaying precisely the "intellectual keenness" and the "spiritual emancipation" from some of the automatic, unexamined values of the community that he had predicted. Furthermore their capacity for doing so was the result, in large part, of the forces he had predicted would bring about an intellectual renascence in the South, and the very university in which he taught and which had helped to educate them was a prime agency of those forces. For most of the twelve southerners were Vanderbilt men, all of them had been born into a society characterized, as Mims put it, by "the sentiment, the chivalry, and the hospitality" (along with a few other things) of the older South, and all had been exposed, at Vanderbilt and elsewhere, to "the intellectual keenness, the spiritual sensitiveness, and the enlarged freedom of the modern world."

The difference was that where Mims and all the other prophets of a modern, enlightened South saw the coming

of modernism to the South of the 1920s as a mostly un-
mixed blessing, the Agrarians thought it contained as
much potentiality for plague as for blessing. Where Mims
and his friends envisioned a relatively painless process
whereby the benefits of urban, industrial enlightenment
were to be united with the more attractive aspects of the
older South's devotion to leisure and individual identity,
the Agrarians foresaw great difficulties. Furthermore the
Agrarian concept of what the good life was all about dif-
fered importantly from that of Mims and the advocates of
Progress. Not only did the Agrarians want to hold onto a
great deal more of the older South's ways of thinking and
feeling, but they stressed the menace that an uncritical
acceptance of the industrial *ethos* posed for "the sentiment,
the chivalry, and the hospitality" that Mims wanted the
South to hold onto. In almost every way the picture of the
South represented by *I'll Take My Stand* represented a far
more searching and pessimistic scrutiny of the changing
nature of southern society than did Mims's book, and dem-
onstrated a much more acute sensitivity to the problems
facing the South of the 1930s. The Agrarians were able, as
Mims and so many other prophets of a new urbanized
South of progress and enlightenment were not, to sense
the precarious nature of the boom times of the 1920s, and
to apprehend the tremendous problems of identity and the
rending conflicts of loyalty that the South was confronting
in its belated reentry into the full current of modern
American life.

The leading Agrarians, it must always be kept in mind,
were poets. John Ransom, Allen Tate, Donald Davidson,
and Robert Penn Warren, who formed the nucleus of the
twelve southerners, had begun as members of the Nashville
Fugitives of the early 1920s, and their entry into social
polemic, however seriously it was undertaken, was a side-
line to their main creative task. They were in the vanguard

of that phenomenon subsequently called the southern literary renascence, whereby, beginning in the middle 1920s, the southern states of the American Union began producing a disproportionate share of the best literature being written in the United States. The erstwhile "Sahara of the Bozart," as H. L. Mencken had called it in 1920 in his famous essay of that title, where "a poet is now almost as rare as an oboe-player, a dry-point etcher or a metaphysician," and where except for James Branch Cabell "you will not find a single southern prose writer who can actually write,"[10] became the scene of literary achievement of national and international renown. The year before *I'll Take My Stand* appeared, for example, William Faulkner published *Sartoris* and *The Sound and the Fury,* and Thomas Wolfe *Look Homeward, Angel.* Robert Penn Warren published his first book, a biography of John Brown. There were first novels by Erskine Caldwell and Hamilton Basso. Cabell published *The Way of Ecben,* Ellen Glasgow *They Stooped to Folly,* Stark Young *River House,* Dubose Heyward *Mamba's Daughters.* There were two novels by T. S. Stribling. Merrill Moore published his first book, *The Noise that Time Makes.* Allen Tate published his biography of Jefferson Davis. All this in one year—1929. Within a few years first books would appear by Caroline Gordon, Katherine Anne Porter, Andrew Nelson Lytle, and Lillian Hellman. Elizabeth Madox Roberts, John Gould Fletcher, Donald Davidson, and John Crowe Ransom were already published authors. The South, which for many decades had been a place of little importance in the literary world, came now into full literary flowering.

The last time that the South had attracted much literary attention had been during the local-color movement of the 1880s and 1890s, when for several decades writing by southern authors had seemed to dominate the literary market place. We may recall Judge Albion Tourgée's comment on that occasion, quoted earlier, to the effect that American literature of the period seemed not only largely southern in spirit but distinctly Confederate in sympathy. But that literary flowering had soon died out, and except for Mark Twain, whose relationship to it was tangential, turned out to have produced little work that had lasted beyond its time for reasons of other than historical interest. This time it was different. The decades that have ensued since the 1920s and 1930s have winnowed the chaff from the wheat, and not all the reputations which seemed so imposing during the period between the two world wars have lasted, but it seems clear that the best writing of Faulkner and his contemporaries will be read for many years to come. As Willard Thorp has expressed it, "Finally the hopes of the defeated ones—Timrod, Hayne, Poe—were realized. At last southern literature had come into its own and was a part of world literature. In the Paris bookstores, alongside the novels of Gide and Mauriac stood *La Route au Tabac, Les Ancêtres,* and *Tandis que j'agonise.*"[11]

From the standpoint of their relationship to the South, what is most noticeable about the southern writers of the 1920s is the extent to which, unlike so much of what had passed for southern literature before their day, their work got beneath the surface to the real issues in southern life. Clearly most of it was not written as defense. If the abjuration to "tell about the South" remained as potent as ever, the question was no longer being interpreted as an obligation to put the South's best foot forward, so far as the image of what went on down there was concerned. Indeed, from the standpoint of many southern apologists, quite the reverse seemed true. The novels of most of the better-known southern authors have been periodically castigated in the southern press for their tendency to show the unpleasant aspects of southern life, to exaggerate, supposedly, the ugliness and to ignore the pleasantness. When one of these southern novelists, William Faulkner, won the Nobel prize, the editor of the leading newspaper in his state called him a propagandist of degradation. When Thomas Wolfe published *Look Homeward, Angel* in 1929, the newspaper in the capital city of his state declared that North Carolina and the South had been spat upon. As for the poets, they were not so often attacked by the newspapers, for the simple reason that they were not read—for they wrote "modern poetry" which was "cerebral" and "difficult" and "obscure," and newspaper editors reared in the tradition of Sidney Lanier and Edgar Guest had no time for that.

The twentieth-century southern author's relationship to the community in which he lived, then, was obviously very different than it had ever been earlier. He wrote about the community, but he did not write *for* the community. Unlike the antebellum southern writers, and unlike most of the local color writers, he felt no compulsion to identify the premises of his art with the social and political objectives of the community. In *I'll Take My Stand,* to be sure, the traditional southern pieties were stressed, but that was a polemical work. Whatever the Agrarians may have thought as polemicists, as artists they were not concerned with prescribing for the South's future welfare. They were involved with imaging human experience, as they saw it around them, and what they focused upon was the clash of the modes of human identity. In Allen Tate's "Ode to the Confederate Dead," a poem written in the late 1920s, the central image was that of a modern southerner standing near the gate at a Confederate cemetery and finding himself unable to manage a creative identification with the dead and their Lost Cause. Each time he attempts imaginatively to cross over the wall that seals him off from the "arrogant circumstance" of the dead, his rhetoric breaks down:

> Turn your eyes to the immoderate past,
> Turn to the inscrutable infantry rising

Demons out of the earth—they will not last,
Stonewall, Stonewall, and the sunken fields of hemp,
Shiloh, Antietam, Malvern Hill, Bull Run.
Lost in that orient of the thick-and-fast
You will curse the setting sun.

Cursing only the leaves crying
Like an old man in a storm

You hear the shout, the crazy hemlocks point
With troubled fingers to the silence which
Smothers you, a mummy, in time.[12]

It is the distance between the modern and the historical
identity that is central to the poem. Tate's essay in *I'll
Take My Stand* presented a program: to seize the tradition
"by violence." The poem, imaged as it is in what is rather
than what should be, captures the separation. It should be
noted that it is precisely this separation that we saw implied in John Wade's imaginary Christmas dinner in his
essay on southern humor, though that was not Wade's intention. Wade's essay represented an assertion of the
Proust scholar's identity with the community that in fact
did not, to the extent that he was a Proust scholar, exist. It
was not a shared community experience in time present
that brought him to the dinner; it was a past identity, the
memory of a common experience that ended when the
scholar had left the community and gone off into the world
of scholarship and ideas.

The southern writers of the renascence were almost all
born within a few years of the turn of the century. They
grew up as the South began its belated entry into the modern world. From their parents, from the public and private
values and loyalties of the community, they inherited the
customs, manners, pieties, and beliefs of an older South.
But the assumptions and the attitudes of that South were
making way for new ideas, attitudes and beliefs; the ways

of thought and the modes of sensibility of the twentieth-century urban, industrial America were penetrating into the hinterlands of the South. As young men and women and as southerners they were the recipients of two different and often contradictory sets of values and attitudes. What they were taught at home to think and to believe was one thing; what they saw going on around them and what they thought about it was something else again. When they left home and went off to college, what they learned there did not serve, as in general it seems to have done for their fathers and grandfathers, to reinforce what had been taught to them as truth at home. Instead it seems to have strengthened and confirmed the forces which were separating them from the old community—forces, one must emphasize, that were already emerging within the community itself.

It has not often been remarked the extent to which the literature of the southern literary renascence was a college- and university-nurtured literature. With only one or two exceptions all the major writers who came into prominence in southern literature after the first world war were college-educated authors. On the Nashville Fugitives, of course, the impact of Vanderbilt University is incalculable, as was the Oxford experience of their mentor, John Crowe Ransom. William Faulkner in Oxford, Mississippi (both through the university and through the influence of his learned friend Phil Stone), Thomas Wolfe at Chapel Hill and Harvard, Eudora Welty at Wisconsin, other authors at other colleges and universities also felt the impact of an education that no longer merely confirmed them in the values of the older southern community.

All in all they were the first generation of young southerners since early in the nineteenth century to be brought into direct contact and confrontation with the vanguard of the most advanced thought and feeling of their times. Neither the rising barrier against new ideas decreed by the need to defend and maintain the South's Peculiar Institution, nor the burdening weight of defeat, occupation, poverty, and emotional shock in the wake of the Civil War, served to ward off the impact of the outside world. Coming out of a society which up into their own time had been insulated against so much that was vital and epoch-making in nineteenth- and early twentieth-century thought and feeling, they found themselves living, thinking, feeling, and beginning to write their stories and poems in the United States of the 1920s. "Equipped with Grecian thoughts," wrote John Ransom in one of his earliest poems, "How could I live / Among my father's folk?"[13] Thomas Wolfe, writing back to his drama teacher at Chapel Hill to describe the experience of the '47 Workshop at Harvard, reported indignantly that one of his fellow graduate students criticized a play as "a perfect illustration of the Freudian complex," instead of saying "that's great stuff" or "rotten" as was done back home.[14] Allen Tate published a poem in the *Double Dealer* and received a letter from Hart Crane, who told him that his poem "showed that I had read Eliot—which I had not done; but I soon did; and my difficulties were enormously increased."[15] Thus was it with the young southerners as they discovered the modern world.

But they did not go into confrontation with that world unarmed. They took with them the experience of the southern community and the southern past, and such experience was, all in all, a formidable legacy of attitudes, presuppositions, and habits of feeling and belief, which was not to be violated without resistance. If the hold of that legacy had weakened before the onslaught of modernity, it was by no means dead. We have seen how, in the instance of Mark Twain, the memory and the attitudes of the life in the Mississippi River town of his youth and boyhood figured in all the art of his later years, and of how the conflicts within the village and river experience and the values and beliefs of his maturity provided the creative tension that he sought to resolve in his fiction. The writers of the twentieth-century South likewise knew the clash of different kinds of experience, and for them the hold of the old ways was if anything even more tenacious and dramatic. For they came to the modern world with the added increment of the defeat and shock that the war had wrought, the heritage of a history that was not merely textbook knowledge but part of the personal experience of their families and their communities, and the physical scars of which had only just been erased even while the psychological markings remained. The South had lost a war. The South had experienced defeat, privation. The South had a past that could not be ignored, and the impact of that past was very real and still very potent. For the young southerners who became the writers of the southern renascence, then, it was impossible to view the present without an awareness of the past that had produced them, and any dream of the future would be tempered by the sobering memory of historical reality. Thus the southern writers were historically minded, to an extent that was true of very little other American writing of their time. They saw things in time, and they did not discount the influence of the past upon the present.

The literature of the twentieth-century South, then, faces two ways: toward the present, and toward the past. The viewpoint of each is made to interpret the other. In Allen Tate's words, "the South not only reentered the world with the first World War; it looked around and saw for the first time since about 1830 that the Yankees were not to blame for everything."[16] Thus the exploration of the past became not merely an exercise in justification, but a search for meaning, which took the searcher down below the surface of the events into their underlying causes, and the result was a literature that at its best illuminated what Faulkner called the "problems of the human heart in conflict with itself."[17] If *Absalom, Absalom!*, to take an example, were merely a fictionalized recital of events in nineteenth-century Mississippi history, it would be as little read today as a book like Mary Johnston's *The Long Roll* or Augusta Evans Wilson's *Macaria*. But, unlike those two authors of an earlier day, Faulkner was not seeking to write a justification of the secession of the southern states. He did not seek to use the southern past to prove to northern readers that the South was not primarily defending human slavery when it went to war in 1861. Instead he sought to understand what the past was, and why it maintained its hold upon the present, and in order to do that he made the effort of Quentin Compson to understand the story of Colonel Thomas Sutpen into an image of man's search for human meaning and definition in his past.

There has been considerable dispute among literary critics as to whether *Absalom, Absalom!* is "about" the South. Critics such as Cleanth Brooks have rightly objected to an easy sociological reading of the story of the rise and fall of the House of Thomas Sutpen as if it were a myth of the fall of the South. Brooks points out, correctly, that Sutpen is in no sense a "typical" antebellum planter, but a parvenu who moved to create for himself a "dynasty" as if it were a disembodied idea; Sutpen's "design" takes precedence over the lives of the people who are involved in it, and he follows out the elements of his design with a most unsouthern calculated abstraction, seizing upon the outward facade of the aristocrat without for a minute accepting the human responsibilities involved. Brooks stresses how Sutpen's insistence upon racial purity, which leads him to reject his son and causes the dynasty to come toppling, does not even rise out of any personal hatred of the black man. He moves entirely in accordance with the demands of the abstract "design," and since in that time and place the demands involved the rejection of Negro blood, he rejects Charles Bon. "He does not hate his first wife or feel repugnance for her child," Brooks declares. "He does not hate just as he does not love. His passion is totally committed to the design. Not even his own flesh and blood are allowed to distract him from that."[18] Brooks also points out that the actual narrative offers little license to regard the details about Sutpen's life and motivations as established fact, for almost everything of importance to the understanding of Sutpen's behavior is conjecture, much of it revealing more about the persons doing the conjecturing than about the events being pondered. The tortuous fabric of inference, assumption, and hunch that Quentin Compson and the Canadian Shreve McCannon weave—the latter without any serious emotional commitment to the story—serves to cloak the sparse structure of known events with a texture of motive and passion that is largely unproven because unprovable.[19]

Brooks's analysis is a needed and healthy corrective to much that has been written about the novel. And he is quite right, I think, in referring to it as being "from one point of view a wonderful detective story," in which we read along to see how Quentin and Shreve make imaginative constructs out of a few given facts, and discover that "much of history is really a kind of imaginative construction."[20] But for all that, one must finally concede that *Absalom, Absalom!* is "about" the South—though certainly not in any literal sense of being a fictionalized illustration of the curse of slavery. It is "about" the South in that it portrays a young southerner coming to grips with the meaning of his community's past. The chronological developments throughout, it must be emphasized, are not that of the history of Thomas Sutpen, but the progress that Quentin Compson is making in finding out and thinking

Thomas Sutpen. From the point at the outset of the novel
in which he sits in Miss Rosa Coldfield's parlor and hears
the old woman begin a story of the long-ago arrival of
Thomas Sutpen into the little community of Jefferson, all
the way through to the end, it is Quentin listening and
talking and surmising. It opens in Jefferson shortly before
Quentin is to leave for college, it ends in the "iron New
England" dark of a bedroom at Harvard as Quentin thinks
of what he has heard and seen and what he has conjectured
as having happened. At the start Quentin is bored and restless, a little impatient at having to listen to the old lady's
story. But by the end of the novel he has become so caught
up himself in the piecing together of the tale, and its implications for himself, that he lies in bed staring at the window, shaking violently and uncontrollably as he remem-
bers the events of the evening in which he accompanied
Miss Rosa out to the rotting mansion in the forest, and the
letter his father has sent informing him of Miss Rosa's
funeral. What began as an old woman's tale of a long-ago
day ends with Quentin so deeply involved in the story that
he can hardly control his own feelings. To repeat, it is
Quentin's story, as Faulkner himself pointed out in a letter to Malcolm Cowley:

> I think Quentin, not Faulkner, is the correct yardstick
> here. I was writing the story, but he not I was brooding
> over a situation. I mean, I was creating him as a character,
> as well as Sutpen et al. He (Quentin) grieved and re-
> gretted the passing of an order the dispossessor of which
> he was not tough enough to withstand. But more he
> grieved the fact (because he hated and feared the porten-
> tous symptom) that a man like Sutpen, who to Quentin
> was trash, originless, could not only have dreamed so high
> but have had the force and strength to have failed so
> grandly.[21]

The "southern" factor, then, is not so much whether Sutpen was or was not an exemplar of a slaveholding and racial injustice, as it is the way in which the history of Thomas Sutpen and what he represented impinges upon the imagination and the conscience of Quentin Compson, a young southerner away at college in New England in the year 1910 (or 1909, depending upon which Faulknerian chronology one uses).

Strictly in point of fact the story of Thomas Sutpen bears a great deal more resemblance to the history of the Deep South (into which Quentin Compson and William Faulkner were both born) than some commentators are willing to admit. For just as Sutpen came there out of obscure origins to set up a plantation, so the Deep South was settled during the 1830s and 1840s not primarily by the descendants of the old Tidewater aristocracy of the eastern seaboard but by "new men," who built their homes almost overnight in what had been wilderness, creating a functioning society of columned mansions and landed estates within the space of a few years. And just as Thomas Sutpen's design for a dynasty came crashing down about him at the end of the Civil War when Henry Sutpen killed his half-brother Charles Bon at his father's behest because "his mother was part Negro," so the society of the Deep South was blasted by the war that was fought to defend a way of life based in important respects on the denial of the black man's humanity. And just as the very strength and will of Thomas Sutpen that had enabled him to create the glory of Sutpen's Hundred out of nothing was also mixed irretrievably with the ruthless capacity for using and then putting aside the human beings who were necessary to make his design come true, so the dream and the achievement of the society of the Deep South were inseparable from the willingness to own human beings as slaves. And finally, just as the heirs of Thomas Sutpen were forced to pay in pain and loss for the human consequences of the design of Thomas Sutpen, so the generation that followed the defeat of the Old South in war were left with the agonizing and desperate consequences of what their forefathers had wrought. All this is history; but more than that it is part of the fibre of Quentin Compson's being.

That a man like Sutpen could act so, and that what he did could have such consequences, that a dream of aristocratic honor could have room in it for what drove and motivated a Thomas Sutpen, that the legacy of grandeur and of failure, pride and guilt, which was Quentin's birthright could involve such extraordinary heroism and terrible evil, was what the untangling of the story of *Absalom, Absalom!* revealed to Quentin Compson. That was why, as he sat down to listen to Miss Rosa talking, "he would seem to listen to two separate Quentins now—the Quentin Compson preparing for Harvard in the South, the deep South dead since 1865 and peopled with garrulous outraged baffled ghosts, listening, having to listen, to one of the ghosts who had refused to lie still longer than most had, telling him about old ghost-times; and the Quentin Compson who was still too young to deserve yet to be a ghost, but nevertheless having to be one for all that, since he was born and bred in the deep South same as she was—the two Quentins now talking to one another in the long silence of notpeople, in notlanguage. . . ."[22]

The modern, twentieth-century southern youth, preparing for college, trying to live in the present and about to disengage himself geographically at least from that community past which was still all around him, and the Quentin who inherited that past and was forever marked by it: he was both of them, and neither would let the other alone. The story that is *Absalom, Absalom!* is the dialogue of that conversation between the two Quentins, and, just so, the literature of the twentieth-century South is the exploration, in love and hate, of the confrontation of the older heritage and the modern circumstance within the imagination of writers. No wonder then, that Quentin, upon hearing Shreve McCannon's absurd formulation of his relationship to his home into a question such as "Why do you hate the South?," responds at once, immediately, "I dont hate it." To comprehend and categorize a relationship as involved and as complex as that between him and his community—between one aspect of his own identity and another in so pat and brutally oversimplified a term as "hate" or "love" is impossible. He both hates it *and* loves it; he both sees its nature and shares in it.

This is why it seems to me legitimate to say that the Quentin Compson of *Absalom, Absalom!* speaks for the southern writer of our time. Moving as he did out of the order and identity of the older southern community into a twentieth-century world with different and often contradictory values and attitudes, he was forced to define himself, in the process of apprehension and discovery that is artistic creation, in terms of those two kinds of knowledge. We can see the same dynamics at work in the writings of all of the southern authors. "What shall we say who have knowledge carried to the heart?" asks the protagonist of Tate's "Ode to the Confederate Dead." He means the memory of an older kind of human identity that did not divide knowledge and feeling into separate and clashing categories; what shall those who possess that memory make of their present, their different and less unified, more fragmented circumstance? It is not a matter of adopting the attitudes of that earlier day as if they were still sufficient and appropriate, for that day is gone. One cannot view the past as that past saw itself. What remains is a *way* of looking, an incapacity for accepting the abstraction and dissociation of modern life as the only thing possible under the circumstances, and yet an awareness of difficulty of doing or seeking otherwise in the conditions of modern society.

Eugene Gant, in Wolfe's *Look Homeward, Angel,* is ready, as the novel closes, to leave the closed, restricted world of the southern mountain city of Altamont forever, to find fulfillment in the shining city of the metropolis beyond. All the same he is not really sure that what he seeks is to be found there, and he admits to his ghostly brother Ben that he may simply be taking a train trip. Thomas Wolfe began *Look Homeward, Angel* while in France, where he was possessed by the thoughts of home, and he painted the people and the place of his origins in a lavishness of what he termed "space, color and time" that gave them a richness of texture that is largely missing in his subsequent portrayals of life in the metropolis and elsewhere. The sense of time flowing all about him, carrying away everything he had known, pervades his work, and so does the sense of history, of the inescapable heritage of the past acting upon the present. And in his last completed work, the novella "The Party at Jack's," later incorporated clumsily by his editor into *You Can't Go Home Again,* he presents an apartment house fire which is made to signify the emptiness, selfishness, and lack of concern that is the life of the wealthy in the metropolis.

In Robert Penn Warren's third and best novel, *All the King's Men,* Jack Burden, scion of an old, aristocratic Louisiana family, moves out of the complacency and sterility of existence at fashionable Burden's Landing to seek a more active and significant kind of life as aide to a redneck politician, Willie Stark, who knows how to manipulate power and get needed things done in a democratic, industrial society. But Willie Stark is too willing to compromise his ideals for the purposes of expediency, and thus the ideals themselves are corrupted, and the result is the downfall of Willie's empire, the death of Willie and of others, and a general breakdown. Only through tragedy can Jack Burden learn that there is no substitute for personal responsibility, no evasion of the individual's need to search out his own moral principles in whatever he does.

In Eudora Welty's *The Golden Apples* the tightly-bound little community of Morgana unites to keep from its consciousness the knowledge of art, morality, heroism, and loneliness that the music teacher Miss Eckhart brings into the community with her. Those who would remain in Morgana can do so only if they give their allegiance to the common conspiracy against that dread knowledge. Because certain of the townsfolk cannot, they must leave, or if they try to remain, be marked by their difference. In *Losing Battles* the schoolteacher Miss Julia Mortimer wages a life-long battle to educate the inhabitants of the community of Banner to the knowledge of their private spiritual hunger, and the community resists the responsibility that such self-knowledge would impose. The clash between the private sensibility and the community identity is developed, sometimes in comedy, sometimes in tragedy, throughout Miss Welty's work.

One could go on to show how the same perception of divided and contradictory modes and attitudes of life and thought provides the dramatic tension in the writings of every one of the twentieth-century southern writers. Each of them makes something different out of it. But in each writer's work, whether in poetry or fiction, it is there. In the novels of William Faulkner, the greatest of all of them, it is displayed most brilliantly and memorably, of course. Faulkner's mighty Yoknapatawpha saga is built squarely upon it. The fall of the great families, the Compsons, Sartorises, De Spains, and the rise of the weasel-like Snopeses with their low cunning and freedom from ethical scruples, could only have been conceived and written by a writer who was intimately involved in the attitudes and values of his community and yet at the same time so distanced from them that he could subject them to devastating critical scrutiny. No writer of Faulkner's generation, for example, has explored, in more detail and with such understanding, the role of the black man in the southern community. Yet he has never seen the problem merely as topical; instead he has used it as symbol of the quest for human identity in society. Thus in *Light in August* the inability and unwillingness of Joe Christmas to accept the arbitrary identity that the community has decreed in terms of being either black or white is made into the struggle of a strong, driven man to assert his individuality in the very face of not only social demarcation but of human limitation itself. Christmas's *I will not serve* becomes more than protest against his society and its restrictions; it is made into a defiance of human despondence, and in seeking his own doom, he does what a man can do. Thus Faulkner, distanced from the community yet apprehending its pull, makes of his "own little postage stamp of native soil"[23] a furnace wherein the tumult and confusion of a changing South become metamorphosed into the struggle of human beings for individual identity in the toils of social and spiritual necessity.

Warren is right: William Faulkner did indeed reenact within his own soul, in vice and virtue, the history of his people. No writer can do more.

Notes

ONE—*The Literary Community in the Old South*

1. William Faulkner, *Absalom, Absalom!* (New York: Random House, 1936), pp. 9–10.

2. Ibid., p. 174.

3. Robert Penn Warren, "Faulkner: The South, the Negro, and Times," in Warren, ed., *Faulkner: A Collection of Critical Essays* (Englewood Cliffs, N.J.: Prentice-Hall, 1966), p. 271.

4. "An Interview with William Styron," in Malcolm Cowley, ed., *Writers at Work: The Paris Review Interviews* (New York: Viking Press, 1959), p. 272.

5. See for example Styron's article, "This Quiet Dust," *Harper's*, cccxx (April 1965), 135–46.

6. Sidney Lanier, Furlow College Address, June 30, 1869; quoted in Jay B. Hubbell, *The South in American Literature, 1607–1900* (Durham: Duke University Press, 1954), p. 762.

7. Frederick L. Gwynn and Joseph Blotner, eds., *Faulkner in the University* (Charlottesville: University of Virginia Press, 1959), pp. 9–10.

8. Charles W. Kent, Preface to Edwin Anderson Alderman and Joel Chandler Harris, eds., *Library of Southern Literature* (Atlanta: Martin and Hoyt, 1909), I, xv.

9. "The Wanderer Back Home," in *Library of Southern Literature,* I, 427.

10. Edwin A. Alderman, Introduction, *Library of Southern Literature,* I, xxi.

11. Quoted in Douglas Southall Freeman, *The South to Posterity* (New York: Charles Scribner's Sons, 1939), p. 49.

12. William P. Trent, *William Gilmore Simms* (Boston and New York: Houghton Mifflin, 1892), p. 246. Hereinafter cited as Trent.

13. Quoted in Curtis Carroll Davis, *That Ambitious Mr. Legaré* (Columbia: University of South Carolina Press, 1971), p. 45.

14. Allen Tate, "The Profession of Letters in the South," *Essays of Four Decades* (Chicago: Swallow Press, 1968), p. 523.

15. *Southern Quarterly Review,* April 1853; quoted in Hubbell, *The South in American Literature,* p. 367.

16. *Southern Literary Messenger,* April 1856; quoted in Hubbell, *The South in American Literature,* p. 341.

17. Henry Timrod, "Literature in the South," in Edd Winfield Parks, ed., *The Essays of Henry Timrod* (Athens: University of Georgia Press, 1942), p. 100.

18. George W. Cable, "The Due Restraints and Liberties of Literature," June 15, 1883; quoted in Arlin Turner, "George W. Cable's Revolt against Literary Sectionalism," *Tulane Studies in English,* v (New Orleans, 1955), 25–26.

19. Joel Chandler Harris, "Literature in the South," *Atlanta Constitution,* November 30, 1879; quoted in Paul M. Cousins, *Joel Chandler Harris* (Baton Rouge: Louisiana State University Press, 1968), p. 109.

20. James Branch Cabell, "Mr. Ritchie's Richmond," *Let Me Lie* (New York: Farrar, Straus, 1947), p. 123.

21. Trent, p. 129.

22. Quoted in Trent, p. 238.

23. William Gilmore Simms, October 30, 1858; quoted in Trent, p. 239.

24. Quoted in Trent, p. 238.

25. Louis D. Rubin, Jr. "Southern Local Color and the Black Man," *Southern Review,* vi, n. s. (Autumn 1970), 1011–30.

26. Paul Hamilton Hayne, to Richard Henry Stoddard, November 7, 1856, in Daniel Morley McKeithan, ed., *A Collection of Hayne Letters* (Austin: University of Texas Press, 1944), pp. 20–21.

27. C. Vann Woodward, "Southern Slaves in the World of Thomas Malthus," *American Counterpoint: Slavery and Racism in the North-South Dialogue* (Boston: Little, Brown, 1971), pp. 84–85.

28. Ibid., p. 105.

29. Eugene Genovese, "The Slave South: An Interpretation," *The Political Economy of Slavery* (New York: Vintage Books, 1967), p. 32.

30. Ibid., p. 28.

31. Ibid., p. 32 ff.

32. Harriet Beecher Stowe, *Uncle Tom's Cabin or, Life Among the Lowly,* ed. Kenneth S. Lynn (Cambridge: Harvard University Press, 1962), p. 455.

33. William Cullen Bryant, "Barnwell District, S.C., March 29th," *A Tour in the Old South,* in *Prose Writings,* ii, ed. Parke Godwin (New York: 1884), p. 34.

34. Quoted in Hubbell, *The South in American Literature,* pp. 584–85.

35. Trent, pp. 142–43.

36. Genovese, "The Slave South: An Interpretation," p. 30.

37. Henry Timrod, "Ethnogenesis," in Edd Winfield Parks and Aileen

Well Parks, eds., *The Collected Poems of Henry Timrod* (Athens: University of Georgia Press, 1965) , p. 95.

38. Woodward, "The Southern Ethic in a Puritan World," *American Counterpoint*, pp. 39–40.

39. Tate, "The Profession of Letters in the South," p. 527.

40. Ibid., p. 529.

41. John B. Cullen, in collaboration with Floyd C. Watkins, *Old Times in the Faulkner Country* (Chapel Hill: University of North Carolina Press, 1961) , p. 54.

42. [William Gilmore Simms], Advertisement, in [Simms, ed.], *The Charleston Book: A Miscellany in Prose and Verse* (Charleston, S.C.: Samuel Hart Sen., 1845) , pp. iii–iv.

43. *Absalom, Absalom!*, p. 378.

TWO—*Mark Twain and the Postwar Scene*

1. Thomas Nelson Page, "Authorship in the South before the War," *The Old South* (New York: Chautauqua Press, 1919) , p. 64.

2. Page, "The Old South," *The Old South*, pp. 25–26, 50.

3. Ibid., p. 51.

4. Albion W. Tourgée, "The South as a Field for Fiction," *Forum*, VI (1886) , 405.

5. Paul H. Buck, *The Road to Reunion* (Boston: Little, Brown, 1937) , p. 235.

6. Robert E. Spiller, *The Cycle of American Literature* (New York: Macmillan, 1955) , p. 185.

7. Henry Timrod, "The Cotton Boll," in Edd Winfield Parks and Aileen Wells Parks, eds., *The Collected Poems of Henry Timrod* (Athens: University of Georgia Press, 1965) , p. 99.

8. [Walter Hines Page], *The Southerner, Being the Autobiography of Nicholas Worth* (New York: Doubleday, Page, 1909) , p. 46.

9. Henry James, *The American Scene*, ed. Leon Edel (Bloomington: Indiana University Press, 1968) , p. 377.

10. Mark Twain, *Life on the Mississippi*, Vol. III, *Complete Works of Mark Twain: Authorized Edition* (New York: Harper and Bros., 1917) , p. 364.

11. [Page], *The Southerner*, p. 46.

12. William Faulkner, *Absalom, Absalom!* New York: Random House, 1936, p. 361.

13. Leslie Fiedler, "Huckleberry Finn: Faust in the Eden of Childhood," *Love and Death in the American Novel* (New York: Criterion Books, 1960) , pp. 553–91.

14. Lewis Leary, "Mark Twain and the Comic Spirit," *Southern Ex-*

cursions: Essays on Mark Twain and Others (Baton Rouge: Louisiana State University Press, 1971) , p. 5.

15. Lewis Leary, Preface, *Southern Excursions,* p. x.

16. William Dean Howells, *My Mark Twain,* in Edmund Wilson, ed., *The Shock of Recognition,* Vol. II (New York: Grosset and Dunlap, 1955) , p. 695.

17. Ibid., p. 740.

18. C. Hugh Holman, *Three Modes of Modern Southern Fiction* (Athens: University of Georgia Press, 1966) , p. 6.

19. Ibid., pp. 55–57.

20. Dixon Wecter, *Sam Clemens of Hannibal* (Boston: Houghton Mifflin, 1952) , p. 209.

21. DeLancey Ferguson, *Mark Twain: Man and Legend* (Indianapolis: Bobbs-Merrill, 1943) , p. 15.

22. Mark Twain, *Mark Twain's Autobiography,* I [no vol. no.], *Complete Works of Mark Twain: Authorized Edition* (New York: Harper and Bros., 1924) , p. 123.

23. James G. Baldwin, *The Flush Times of Alabama and Mississippi* (New York: Sagamore Press, 1957) , p. 66.

24. Wecter, *Sam Clemens of Hannibal,* pp. 74–76.

25. Ibid., p. 77.

26. Mark Twain, *Life on the Mississippi,* Vol. VII, *Complete Works of Mark Twain: Authorized Edition* (New York: Harper and Bros., 1924) , p. 122.

27. Quoted in Henry Nash Smith, *Mark Twain: The Development of a Writer* (Cambridge: Harvard University Press, 1962) , p. 93.

28. Quoted in Guy A. Cardwell, *Twins of Genius* (London: Neville Spearman, 1962) , p. 25.

29. Justin Kaplan, *Mr. Clemens and Mark Twain* (New York: Simon and Schuster, 1966) , p. 353.

30. Ibid., p. 380.

31. Mark Twain, "The Last Lotus Club Speech," in *Mark Twain's Speeches,* Vol. XXIV, *Complete Works of Mark Twain: Authorized Edition* (New York: Harper and Bros., 1923) , pp. 373–74.

32. Quoted in Wecter, *Sam Clemens of Hannibal,* p. 67.

33. Mark Twain, *Pudd'nhead Wilson and Those Extraordinary Twins.* Facsimile of the First Edition (San Francisco: Chandler Publishing Co., 1968) , p. 156.

34. Wecter, *Sam Clemens of Hannibal,* pp. 69–71.

35. Mark Twain, *The Adventures of Huckleberry Finn,* Introduction by Lionel Trilling (New York: Rinehart, 1948) , p. 105.

36. Bernard DeVoto, "Symbols of Despair," *Mark Twain at Work* (Cambridge: Harvard University Press, 1942) , p. 116.

37. Albert Bigelow Paine, *Mark Twain: A Biography,* Vol. I (New York: Harper and Bros., 1912) , pp. 74–75.

38. Wecter, *Sam Clemens of Hannibal*, pp. 117–18.

39. Smith, *Mark Twain: The Development of a Writer*.

40. Mark Twain, "No. 44, The Mysterious Stranger," in *Mark Twain's Mysterious Stranger Manuscripts*, ed. William M. Gibson (Berkeley and Los Angeles: University of California Press, 1969), p. 405.

41. Lionel Trilling, Introduction, *The Adventures of Huckleberry Finn*, p. xviii.

42. William Faulkner, *Light in August* (New York: Modern Library, 1950), p. 426.

43. Holman, *Three Modes of Modern Southern Fiction*, p. 53.

44. *Life on the Mississippi*, p. 376.

45. *Adventures of Huckleberry Finn*, p. 14.

46. Ibid., p. 146.

47. *Life on the Mississippi*, p. 377.

48. Ibid., p. 259.

49. Samuel Langhorne Clemens, *A Connecticut Yankee in King Arthur's Court*, Facsimile of the First Edition (San Francisco: Chandler Publishing Co., 1963), p. 28.

50. Ibid., pp. 515–16.

51. Smith, *Mark Twain: The Development of a Writer*, p. 170. Smith's more extensive analysis of *A Connecticut Yankee* is *Mark Twain's Fable of Progress* (New Brunswick: Rutgers University Press), 1964.

52. *Life on the Mississippi*, p. 375.

53. *A Connecticut Yankee*, p. 262.

54. Ibid., p. 387.

55. Ibid., p. 363.

56. Ibid., pp. 361–62.

57. Mark Twain, "Villagers of 1840–3," in *Mark Twain's Hannibal, Huck and Tom*, ed. Walter Blair (Berkeley and Los Angeles: University of California Press, 1969), p. 43.

58. James M. Cox, *Mark Twain: The Fate of Humor* (Princeton University Press, 1966), p. 196.

59. Mark Twain, *The Adventures of Tom Sawyer*, Vol. I, *Complete Works of Mark Twain* (New York: Harper and Bros., 1922), p. 292.

60. *Life on the Mississippi*, p. 142.

61. For a discussion of the imagery of the Quarles Farm in Clemens's fiction, see Smith, *Mark Twain: The Development of a Writer*, pp. 129–32.

62. *Pudd'nhead Wilson*, p. 142.

63. Mark Twain, "Jane Lampson Clemens," in *Mark Twain's Hannibal, Huck and Tom*, ed. Blair, p. 46.

64. Mark Twain, "On Lincoln's Birthday," in *Mark Twain's Speeches*, p. 231.

65. Ibid., p. 230.

THREE—*The Writer in the Twentieth-Century South*

1. John Donald Wade, "Southern Humor," in *Culture in the South,* ed. W. T. Couch (Chapel Hill: University of North Carolina Press, 1934), pp. 616–28.

2. Ibid., p. 624.

3. Ibid., p. 626.

4. Allen Tate, "Remarks on the Southern Religion," in Twelve Southerners, *I'll Take My Stand: The South and the Agrarian Tradition* (New York: Harper and Bros., 1962), p. 174.

5. [John Crowe Ransom], "Introduction: A Statement of Principles," *I'll Take My Stand,* p. xxix.

6. Robert Penn Warren, in Rob Roy Purdy, ed., *Fugitives' Reunion: Conversations at Vanderbilt* (Nashville: Vanderbilt University Press, 1959), pp. 209–10.

7. Ibid., p. 213.

8. George B. Tindall, *The Emergence of the New South, 1913–1945* (Baton Rouge: Louisiana State University Press, 1967), p. 56.

9. Edwin Mims, *The Advancing South* (New York: Doubleday, Page, 1926), pp. 315–16.

10. H. L. Mencken, "The Sahara of the Bozart," *Prejudices: Second Series.* New York: Knopf, 1920), p. 136 ff.

11. Willard Thorp, "The Arts: Writing," *A Southern Reader* (New York: Knopf, 1955), p. 649.

12. Allen Tate, "Ode to the Confederate Dead," *Poems 1922–1947* (New York: Charles Scribner's Sons, 1948), p. 22.

13. John Crowe Ransom, "The School," *Poems About God* (New York: Holt, 1919), p. 72.

14. Thomas Wolfe, Letter to Frederick H. Koch, November 28, 1920, in *The Letters of Thomas Wolfe,* ed. Elizabeth Nowell (New York: Charles Scribner's Sons, 1956), p. 10.

15. Allen Tate, "*The Fugitive* 1922–1925: A Personal Recollection Twenty Years Later," *Princeton University Library Chronicle,* III, 3 (April 1942), 80–81.

16. Allen Tate, "A Southern Mode of the Imagination," *Essays of Four Decades* (Chicago: Swallow Press, 1968), p. 592.

17. William Faulkner, "Address upon Receiving the Nobel Prize for Literature," in *William Faulkner: Essays, Speeches and Public Letters,* ed. James B. Meriwether (New York: Random House, 1965), p. 119.

18. Cleanth Brooks, *William Faulkner: The Yoknapatawpha Country* (New Haven: Yale University Press, 1966), p. 299.

19. Ibid., pp. 295–324. Not the least fascinating part of Brooks's discussion is the material in the appendix, pp. 424–43, in particular the

lengthy tabulation of which character knows which "facts" about what happened, and what is his authority for so knowing.

20. Ibid., p. 311.

21. William Faulkner, Letter to Malcolm Cowley, November 1948, in Malcolm Cowley, *The Faulkner-Cowley File: Letters and Memories, 1944–1962* (New York: Viking Press, 1966), p. 15.

22. William Faulkner, *Absalom, Absalom!* (New York: Random House, 1936), p. 9.

23. "William Faulkner: an Interview," with Jean Stein, in *Writers at Work: The Paris Review Interviews*, ed. Malcolm Cowley (New York: Viking Press, 1959), p. 141.

Index